THE SERMONS OF
HENRY SMITH

THE
SILVER-TONGUED PREACHER

T0371041

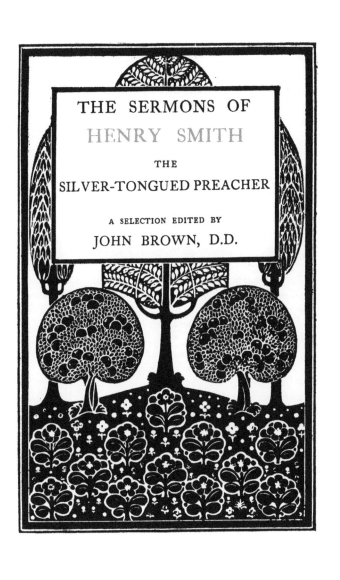

THE SERMONS OF
HENRY SMITH
THE
SILVER-TONGUED PREACHER

A SELECTION EDITED BY
JOHN BROWN, D.D.

CAMBRIDGE UNIVERSITY PRESS
Cambridge, New York, Melbourne, Madrid, Cape Town,
Singapore, São Paulo, Delhi, Mexico City

Cambridge University Press
The Edinburgh Building, Cambridge CB2 8RU, UK

Published in the United States of America by Cambridge University Press, New York

www.cambridge.org
Information on this title: www.cambridge.org/9781107655584

First published 1908
First paperback edition 2013

A catalogue record for this publication is available from the British Library

ISBN 978-1-107-65558-4 Paperback

CONTENTS

CONTENTS

INTRODUCTION

HENRY SMITH, who is apostrophised in Piers
Penniless's *Supplication* (1592) as Silver-tongued
Smith, was a celebrated preacher in Elizabethan
London at St Clement Danes. On leaving
Queens' College, Cambridge, he continued his
studies with Richard Greenham, rector of Dry
Drayton, Cambridgeshire, who imbued him with
Puritan principles as he did other leading men
of the time. In 1575 he also entered Lincoln
College, Oxford, graduating in 1579.

Though as the eldest son and heir of Erasmus
Smith of Somerby and Husbands Bosworth,
Leicestershire, he was heir-apparent to a large
patrimony, he prepared to enter the Ministry of
the Church, but, owing to conscientious scruples
on the matter of subscription, he determined not
to undertake a pastoral charge, but to content
himself with a Lectureship. Strype, in his Life of
Bishop Aylmer, speaks of Smith as " an eloquent
and witty man who in 1587 became Reader or
Lecturer at St Clement Danes, at the desire of
many of the parishioners, and by the favour of
the Lord Treasurer who dwelt in the same parish
and yielded contribution to him."

Thomas Fuller also, in a Life of Henry Smith
which he prefixed to the first Collected Edition of
his works, said of him: " He was commonly
called the Silver-tongued preacher, and that was

but one metal below St Chrysostom himself. His
Church was so crowded with auditors that persons
of good quality brought their own pews with them,
I mean their legs, to stand thereupon in the
alleys. Their ears did so attend to his lips, their
hearts to their ears, that he held the rudder of
their affections in his hands, so that he could
steer them whither he was pleased." Wood, too,
tells us that Smith was "esteemed the miracle
and wonder of his age, for his prodigious memory
and for his fluent, eloquent and practical way of
preaching." (*Athenae Oxon.* i. 603.) And in our
own time Marsden, in his History of the Puritans,
has described Smith's Sermons as "noble examples
of English prose and pulpit eloquence, and as
being free in an astonishing degree from the
besetting vices of his age—vulgarity and quaint-
ness and affected learning."

Owing to ill-health he resigned his Lectureship
about the end of 1590, and retired to Husbands
Bosworth, where he died the following summer,
and was buried July 4th, 1591.

His *Collected* Sermons passed through the
following editions:—1592-3-4-5, 1599, 1604, 1607,
1609, 1612, 1613, 1614, 1617-19, 1620-2, and
1631-2.

J. B.

November, 1908

THE WEDDING GARMENT

Put ye on the Lord Jesus Christ.—Rom. xiii. 14.

THERE be many fashions of apparel, but they
are too light, or too heavy, or too coarse, or too
stale, and all wear out. At last the apostle found
a fashion that surpasseth them all; it is never out
of fashion, meet for all seasons, fit for all persons,
and such a profitable weed, that the more it is
worn the fresher it is. What fashion have you
seen comparable to this? It is not like the clothes
of David's ambassadors, which covered their upper
parts, 2 Sam. x. 4; nor like Saul's armour, which
tired David when he should fight with it, 1 Sam.
xvii. 39; nor like the counterfeit Jeroboam's wife,
which disguised herself to go unknown, 1 Kings
xiv. 2; nor like the old rags of the Gibeonites,
which deceived Joshua, Joshua ix. 4, 5; nor like
the paltry suit of Micah, which he gave once a
year to his Levite, Judges xvii. 10; nor like the
glutton's flaunt, which jetted in purple every day;
nor like the light clothes which Christ said are in
kings' courts, and make them lighter that wear

B.   I   I

them, Mat. xi. 8. But it is like the garment of the
high priests, which had all the names of the tribes
of Israel written upon his breast, Exod. xxviii. 21;
so all the names of the faithful are written in the
breast of Christ, and registered in the book of his
merits, Mal. iii. 16. It is like Elias's mantle,
which divided the waters, 2 Kings ii. 8; so he
divided our sins and punishments, that they which
are clothed with Christ, are armed both against sin
and death. It is like the garments of the Israelites
in the wilderness, which did not wear; forty years
together they wandered in the desert, and yet, saith
Moses, their shoes were not worn, but their apparel
was as when they came out of Egypt, Deut. xxix.
5; so the righteousness of Christ doth last for ever,
and his merits are never worn out.

This garment Paul hath sent unto you, to go
before the king of heaven and earth, a holy garment, a royal garment, an immaculate garment,
an everlasting garment; a garment whereof every
hem is peace of conscience, every plait is joy
in the Holy Ghost, every stitch is the remission
of some sin, and saveth him which weareth it. If
we put on Christ, we are clothed with his obedience, whereby our wickedness is covered; we are
clothed with his merits, whereby our sins are forgiven; we are clothed with his Spirit, whereby our
hearts are mollified, and sanctified, and renewed,

2

till we resemble Christ himself. This is the apostle's meaning, to put on Christ, as it is unfolded in Col. iii. 12. Where he brings forth all the robes of Christ, and sorts of them, and saith, Put on mercy, put on meekness, put on humility, put on patience, put on love; all which before he called the new man. So that to put on Christ, is to put on the new man with all his virtues, until we be renewed to the image of Christ, which is like a new man amongst men. They which labour to be righteous, and yet believe that Christ's righteousness shall save them, have put on Christ as Paul would have them. We are not taught to put on angels, nor saints, nor the Virgin Mary, nor Paul himself, to cover our sins with their righteousness, as the papists do ; but we are commanded to put on Christ, and cover our sins with his righteousness. The body hath many garments, but the soul hath one garment. Every clout will cover our sores, but the finest silk will not cover our sins. Therefore when we seem brave to others, we seem foul to God, because his eye is upon our sins, which lie naked when all the rest is covered, until we put on Christ, and then we hear the voice, 'Thy sins are forgiven,' and we have the blessing, 'Blessed is the man whose sin is covered.' So we are clothed and blessed together.

Now let us see how to put this garment on. Many fumble about it, like children which have need of one to put on their clothes. Some put on Christ like a precious head-tire, which all day is worn, beautified with jewels, and beset with gems, to make the face seem more amiable; but at night that riches is laid aside, and the head muffled with some regardless tire. Thus do our curious women put on Christ, who when they hear the messengers of grace offering this garment, and preparing to make the body fit to be garnished with so glorious a vesture, as Paul did the Romans, first washing away drunkenness and gluttony, then chambering and wantonness, then strife and envy, and so sin after sin, they seem like the stony ground to receive it with joy, and think to beautify their heads with this precious ointment; but when he tells them there is no communion between Christ and Belial, that if this garment be put on, all other vanities must be put off; they then turn their day into darkness, and reject Christ, that would be an eternal crown of beauty to their heads, and wrap their temples in the uncomely rags and refuse of every nation's pride; and in these toys they cause their servants to spend many hours on every day in the week, but especially on the Sabbath day, to deck their bodies, as if they were but little children, which

4

had need of one to put on their clothes. Some put on Christ as a cloak, which hangeth upon their shoulders, and covereth them: when they go abroad to be seen of men, they can cast on the cloak of holiness, and seem for a while as holy as the best; but so soon as they come home the cloak goeth off, and the man is as he was, whose vizard was better than his face. Thus hypocrites put on Christ, as many retain unto noblemen, not to do them any service, but to have their countenance. Many put on Christ like a hat, which goeth off to every one which meets them; so every temptation which meets them, makes them forget what they heard, what they promised, what they resolved, and change their way as though they had not repented at all. So the common people (like yourselves) put on Christ: they are zealous so long as they are in the church, and beat their breasts, and cast up their eyes like the publican, Luke xviii. 13, when they hear a sentence which moves them; as though they would do no more against that saying whiles they live; but the next business putteth all out of mind till they come to the church again. Some put on Christ as a glove, which covereth but the hand; so they put on the face of Christ, or the tongue of Christ; but their hands work, and their feet walk, as they did before. So many professors of religion put on Christ,

5

which call but for discipline and reformation, that they might get a name of zeal and sincerity to cover some fault which they would not be suspected of. Thus every man would cover himself with Christ, but they have not the skill, or they have not the will to put him on.

Now hear how Christ must be put on. As the angel taught John to read the book when he bade him eat it, so must we put on Christ, as if we did eat him. As the meat is turned into the substance of the body and goeth through every part of man, so Christ and his word should go from part to part till we be of one nature with them.

Thus we must put on Christ; for the word signifieth to put him on, as thou wouldest put him in, that he may be one with thee, and thou with him, as it were in a body together. As he hath put on all our infirmities, so we must put on all his graces, not half on, but all on, and clasp him to us, and gird him about us, and wear him, even as we wear our skin, which is alway about us. Then there shall be no need of wires, nor curls, nor periwigs; the husbands shall not be forced to rack their rents, nor enhance their fines, nor sell their lands to deck their wives; but as the poor mantle of Elijah seemed better to Elisha than all the robes of Solomon, 2 Kings ii. 13, so the wedding garment shall seem better than all the flaunts of vanity, and put every fashion out of fashion, which is not modest and comely like itself.

Thus have you heard what is meant by putting on Christ: first, to clothe ourselves with righteousness and holiness like Christ; and then, because our own righteousness is too short to cover our arms, and legs, and thighs of sin, but still some bare place will peer out, and shame us in the sight of God, therefore we must borrow Christ's garments, as Jacob did his brother's, Gen. xxvii. 15, and cover ourselves with his righteousness; that is, believe that his righteousness shall supply our unrighteousness, and his sufferings shall stand for our sufferings, because he came to fulfil the law, and bear the curse, and satisfy his Father for us, that all which believe in him might not die, but have life everlasting, John iii. 16.

Now I have shewed you this goodly garment, you must go to another to help you to put it on; and none can put this garment upon you, but he which is the garment, the Lord Jesus Christ. Therefore to him let us pray.

Thou must put him on as *Lord*; that is, thy ruler to command thee, thy tutor to govern thee, and thy master to direct thee; thou must be no man's servant but his, take no man's part against him, but say with the apostles, 'Whether is it meet to obey God or thee?' Acts iv. 19. Thou must put him on as *Jesus*, that is, thy Saviour in whom thou trustest, thy protector on whom thou dependest, thy Redeemer on whom thou believest; thou must not look for thy salvation from angel, nor saint, nor anything beside him. For the name of Jesus signifieth a Saviour, which is given to none but him, and he is not only called the *Saviour*, but the *Salvation*, in the Song of Simeon, Luke i. 69, to shew that he is the only Saviour; for there be many saviours, but there can be but one salvation; as there may be many tortures, and yet but one death. Therefore, when he is called the *Salvation*, it implieth that there is no saviour beside him. Thou must put him on as *Christ*, that is, a king to rule, a prophet to teach, a priest to pray and sacrifice, and pacify the wrath of God for thee. For this name Christ doth signify that he was anointed a king, a priest, and a prophet for man: a king to rule him, a priest to offer sacrifice for him, a prophet to teach him. So that he putteth on Christ as *Lord*, which worshippeth none but him; he putteth on Christ as *Jesus*, which believeth in none but him; and he putteth on Christ as *Christ*, which worshippeth none but him, believeth in none but him, and heareth none but him.

8

A PREPARATIVE TO MARRIAGE

YOU are come hither to be contracted in the Lord; that is, of two to be made one, Gen. ii. 18; for as God hath knit the bones and sinews together for the strengthening of men's bodies, so he hath knit man and woman together for the strengthening of their life, because 'two are firmer than one,' Eccles. iv. 9. And therefore, when God made the woman for man, he said, 'I will make him an help,' shewing that man is stronger by his wife. Every marriage, before it be knit, should be contracted, as it is shewed in Exod. xxii. 16, and Deut. xxii. 28: which stay between the contract and the marriage was the time of longing, for their affection to settle in, because the deferring of that which we love doth kindle the desire, which, if it came easily and speedily unto us, would make us set less by it. Therefore we read how Joseph and Mary were contracted before they were married, Mat. i. 18. In the contract Christ was conceived, and in the marriage Christ was born, that he might honour both estates: virginity with his conception, and marriage with his birth. You

9

are contracted, but to be married. Therefore I pass from contracts to speak of marriage, which is nothing else but a communion of life between man and woman joined together according to the ordinance of God.

First, I will shew the excellency of marriage; then the institution of it; then the causes of it; then the choice of it; then the duties of it; and lastly, the divorcement of it.

Well might Paul say, Heb. xiii. 4, 'marriage is honourable'; for God hath honoured it himself. It is honourable for the author, honourable for the time, and honourable for the place. Whereas all other ordinances were appointed of God by the hands of men, or the hands of angels, Acts xii. 7, Heb. ii. 2, marriage was ordained by God himself, which cannot err. No man nor angel brought the wife to the husband, but God himself, Gen. ii. 22; so marriage hath more honour of God in this than all other ordinances of God beside, because he solemnized it himself.

Then it is honourable for the time, for it was the first ordinance that God instituted, even the first thing which he did, after man and woman were created, and that in the state of innocency, before either had sinned: like the finest flower, which will not thrive but in a clean ground. Before man had any other calling, he was called to be an husband; therefore it hath the honour of antiquity above all other ordinances, because it was ordained first, and is the ancientest calling of men.

To honour marriage more yet, or rather to teach the married how to honour one another, it is said that the wife was made of the husband's rib, Gen. ii. 22; not of his head, for Paul calleth the husband the wife's head, Ephes. v. 23; not of the foot, for he must not set her at his foot. The servant is appointed to serve, and the wife to help. If she must not match with the head, nor stoop at the foot, where shall he set her then? He must set her at his heart, and therefore she which should lie in his bosom was made in his bosom, and should be as close to him as his rib, of which she was fashioned.

Lastly, in all nations the day of marriage was reputed the joyfullest day in all their life, and is reputed still of all; as though the sun of happiness began that day to shine upon us, when a good wife is brought unto us. Therefore one saith, that marriage doth signify merry-age, because a play-fellow is come to make our age merry, as Isaac and Rebekah sported together.

Solomon considering all these excellencies, as though we were more indebted unto God for this than other temporal gifts, saith, ' Houses and riches are the inheritance of the father, but a prudent wife cometh of the Lord,' Prov. xix. 14.

Houses and riches are given of God, and all things else, and yet he saith, houses and riches are given of parents, but a good wife is given of God, as though a good wife were such a gift as we should account comes from God alone, and accept it as if he should send us a present from heaven, with this name written on it, *the gift of God.*

Beasts are ordained for food, and clothes for warmth, and flowers for pleasure, but the wife is ordained for man; like little Zoar, a city of refuge to fly to in all his troubles, Gen. xix. 20; and there is no peace comparable unto her but the peace of conscience.

Now it must needs be, that marriage, which was ordained of such an excellent author, and in such a happy place, and of such an ancient time, and after such a notable order, must likewise have special causes for the ordinance of it. Therefore the Holy Ghost doth shew us three causes of this union.

One is, the propagation of children, signified in that when Moses saith, Gen. i. 27, 'He created them male and female,' not both male nor both female, but one male and the other female; as if he created them fit to propagate other. And therefore when he had created them so, to shew that propagation of children is one end of marriage, he said unto them, 'Increase and multiply,' Gen. i. 28; that is, bring forth children, as other creatures bring forth their kind.

For this cause marriage is called *matrimony*, which signifieth *motherage*, because it maketh them mothers which were virgins before, and is the seminary of the world, without which all things should be in vain, for want of men to use them; for God reserveth the great city to himself; and this suburbs he hath set out unto us, which are regents by sea and by land.

The second cause is to avoid fornication. This Paul signifieth when he saith, 'For the avoiding of fornication, let every man have his own wife,' 1 Cor. vii. 8. He saith not for avoiding of adultery, but for avoiding of fornication, shewing that fornication is unlawful.

The third cause is to avoid the inconvenience of solitariness, signified in these words, 'It is not good for man to be alone'; as though he had said, This life would be miserable and irksome, and unpleasant to man, if the Lord had not given him a wife to company his troubles. If it be not good for man to be alone, then it is good for man to have a fellow; therefore as God created a pair of all other kinds, so he created a pair of this kind.

13

We say that one is none, because he cannot be fewer than one, he cannot be less than one, he cannot be weaker than one, and therefore the wise man saith, Eccles. iv. 10, 'Woe to him that is alone,' that is, he which is alone shall have woe. Thoughts, and cares, and fears will come to him because he hath none to comfort him, as thieves steal in when the house is empty; like a turtle which hath lost his mate; like one leg when the other is cut off; like one wing when the other is clipped; so had the man been, if the woman had not been joined to him; therefore for mutual society, God coupled two together, that the infinite troubles which lie upon us in the world might be eased with the comfort and help one of another, and that the poor in the world might have some comfort as well as the rich; for 'the poor man,' saith Solomon, 'is forsaken of his own brethren,' Prov. xix. 7; yet God hath provided one comfort for him, like Jonathan's armour-bearer, that shall never forsake him, 1 Sam. xiv. 7, that is, another self, which is the only commodity (as I may term it) wherein the poor do match the rich; without which some persons should have no helper, no comfort, no friend at all.

But as it is not good to be alone, so Solomon sheweth that 'it is better to be alone than to dwell with a froward wife,' Prov. xxi. 9, which is like a quotidian ague, to keep his patience in ure. Such furies do haunt some men, like Saul's spirit, 1 Sam. xvi. 14, as though the devil had put a sword into their hands to kill themselves; therefore choose whom thou mayest enjoy, or live alone still, and thou shalt not repent thee of thy bargain.

That thou mayest take and keep without repentance, now we will speak of the choice, which some call the way to good wives' dwelling, for these flowers grow not on every ground; therefore they say, that in wiving and thriving a man should take counsel of all the world, lest he light upon a curse while he seeks for a blessing. As Moses considered what spies he sent into Canaan, Deut. i. 23, so thou must regard whom thou sendest to spy out a wife for thee. Discretion is a wary spy, but fancy is a rash spy, and liketh whom she will mislike again.

To direct thee to a right choice herein, the Holy Ghost gives thee two rules in the choice of a wife, godliness and fitness; godliness, because our spouse must be like Christ's spouse, that is, graced with gifts and embroidered with virtues, as if we married holiness itself. Secondly, the mate must be fit. It is not enough to be virtuous but to be suitable; for divers women have many

15

virtues, and yet do not fit to some men; and
divers men have many virtues, and yet do not fit
to some women; and therefore we see many
times even the godly couples to jar when they
are married, because there is some unfitness
between them, which makes odds. What is
odds, but the contrary to even? therefore make
them even, saith one, and there will be no odds.
From hence came the first use of the ring in
weddings, to represent this evenness; for if it
be straiter than the finger it will pinch, and if it
be wider than the finger it will fall off, but if it be
fit it neither pincheth nor slippeth; so they which
are alike, strive not; but they which are unlike,
are fire and water. Therefore one observeth, that
concord is nothing but likeness; and all that strife
is for unfitness, as in things when they fit not
together, and in persons when they suit not one
another. How was God pleased when he had
found a king according to his own heart? 1 Sam.
ii. 35. So shall that man be pleased that finds a
wife according to his own heart; whether he be
rich or poor, his peace shall afford him a cheerful
life, and teach him to sing, 'In love is no lack.'
Therefore a godly man in our time thanked the
Lord that he had not only given him a godly
wife, but a fit wife; for he had said, not that she
was the wisest, nor the holiest, nor the humblest,

nor the modestest wife in the world, but the fittest wife for him in the world, which every man should think when that knot is tied, or else so oft as he seeth a better, he will wish that his choice were to make again. As he did thank God for sending him a fit wife, so the unmarried should pray to God to send him a fit wife; for if they be not like, they will not like.

There be certain signs of this fitness and godliness, both in the man and in the woman. If thou wilt know a godly man, or a godly woman, thou must mark five things: the report, the looks, the speech, the apparel, and the companions, which are like the pulses, that shew whether we be well or ill. The report, because as the market goes, so, they say, the market-men will talk. A good man commonly hath a good name, Prov. x. 7, because a good name is one of the blessings which God promiseth to good men.

The next sign is the look; for Solomon saith in Eccles. viii. 1, 'Wisdom is in the face of a man'; so godliness is in the face of a man, and so folly is in the face of a man, and so wickedness is in the face of a man. And therefore it is said in Isa. iii. 9, 'The trial of their countenance testifieth against them'; as though their looks could speak. And therefore we read of 'proud looks,' and 'angry looks,' and 'wanton looks,' because they bewray pride, and anger, and wantonness.

I have heard one say, that a modest man dwells at the sign of a modest countenance; and an honest woman dwelleth at the sign of an honest face, which is like the gate of the temple that was called Beautiful, Acts iii. 2; shewing, that if the entry be so beautiful, within is great beauty. To shew how a modest countenance and womanly shamefacedness do commend a chaste wife, it is observed that the word *nuptiæ*, which signifieth the marriage of the woman, doth declare the manner of her marriage; for it importeth a covering, because the virgins which should be married, when they came to their husbands, for modesty and shamefacedness did cover their faces, as we read of Rebekah, Gen. xxiv. 65, which so soon as she saw Isaac, and knew that he should be her husband, she cast a veil before her face, shewing that modesty should be learned before marriage, which is the dowry that God addeth to her portion.

The third thing is her speech, or rather her silence, for the ornament of a woman is silence; and therefore the law was given to the man rather than to the woman, to shew that he should be the teacher and she the hearer. Solomon describing a right wife saith, 'She openeth her mouth with wisdom and the law of grace is in her tongue.' A wife that can speak this language, is better than she that hath all the tongues.

The fourth sign is the apparel; for as the pride of the glutton is noted, in that he went in purple every day, Luke xvi. 19, so the humility of John is noted, Mark i. 6, in that he went in hair-cloth every day. A modest woman is known by her sober attire, as the prophet Elijah was known by his rough garment, 2 Kings i. 8. Look not for better within than thou seest without, for every one seemeth better than she is; if the face be vanity, the heart is pride.

The fifth sign is the company; for birds of a feather will fly together, and fellows in sin will be fellows in league, even as young Rehoboam chose young companions, 1 Kings xii. 8. The tame beasts will not keep with the wild, nor the clean dwell with the leprous. If a man can be known by nothing else, then he may be known by his companions; for like will to like.

All these properties are not spied at three or four comings, for hypocrisy is spun with a fine thread, and none are deceived so often as lovers. He which will know all his wife's qualities before he be married to her, must see her eating, and walking, and working, and playing, and talking, and laughing, and chiding, or else he shall have less with her than he looked for, or more than he wished for.

When these rules are warily observed, they may join together, and say, as Laban and Bethuel said, Gen. xxiv. 50, 'This cometh of the Lord, therefore we will not speak against it.' How happy are those, in whom faith, and love, and godliness are married together, before they marry themselves! For none of these martial, and cloudy, and whining marriages can say, that godliness was invited to their bridal, and therefore the blessings which are promised to godliness do fly from them.

In Mat. xxii. Christ sheweth, that before parties married, they were wont to put on fair and new garments, which were called wedding-garments; a warning unto all which put on wedding-garments, to put on truth and holiness too, which so precisely is resembled by that garment more than other. Miserable is that man which is fettered with a woman that liketh not his religion; she will be nibbling at his prayers, and at his study, and at his meditations, till she have tired his devotion, and turned the edge of his soul, as David was tried of his malapert Michal: she mocked him for his zeal and liked herself in her folly, 2 Sam. vi. 16; many have fallen at this stone. Therefore, be not wedded to her which hath not the wedding-garment; but let unity go first, and let union follow after, and hope not to convert her, but fear that she will pervert thee, lest thou say after, like him which should come to the Lord's banquet, 'I have married a wife, and cannot come,' Luke xiv. 20.

Yet the chiefest point is behind, that is, our duties. The duties of marriage may be reduced to the duties of man and wife, one toward another, and their duties toward their children, and their duty toward their servants. For themselves, saith one, they must think themselves like to birds: the one is the cock, and the other is the hen; the cock flieth abroad to bring in, and the dam sitteth upon the nest to keep all at home. So God hath made the man to travel abroad, and the woman to keep house; and so their nature, and their wit, and their strength are fitted accordingly; for the man's pleasure is most abroad, and the woman's within.

Love is the marriage virtue which sings music to their whole life.

Wedlock is made of two loves, which I may call the first love and the after love. As every man is taught to love God before he be bid to love his neighbour, so they must love God before they can love one another.

To shew the love which should be between man and wife, marriage is called *conjugium*, which signifieth a knitting or joining together; shewing, that unless there be a joining of hearts, and a knitting of affections together, it is not marriage in deed, but in show and name, and they shall dwell in a house like two poisons in the stomach, and one shall ever be sick of another.

Therefore, first, that they may love, and keep love one with another, it is necessary that they both love God, and as their love increaseth toward him, so it shall increase each to other.

To pass over sleights, which seldom prosper unless they have some warrant, the best policy in marriage is to begin well; for as boards well joined at the first fit close ever after, but if they square not at the first they warp more and more, so they which are well joined are well married; but they which offend their love before it is settled, fade every day like a marigold, which closeth her flower as the sun goeth down, till they hate one another more than they loved at first.

To begin this concord well, it is necessary to learn one another's natures, and one another's affections, and one another's infirmities, because ye must be helpers, and ye cannot help unless you know the disease. All the jars almost which do trouble this band do rise of this, that one doth not hit the measure of the other's heart, apply themselves to either's nature, whereby it cometh to pass that neither can refrain when either is offended, but one sharpeneth another when they had need to be calmed. Therefore they must learn of Paul, 1 Cor. ix. 20, to fashion themselves one to another, if they would win one another; for if any jar do arise, one saith, in no wise divide beds for it, for then the sun goeth down upon their wrath, Eph. iv. 26, and the means of reconcilement is taken away. Give passions no time; for if some men's anger stand but a night, it turneth to malice, which is incurable.

The apostle saith that there will be offences in the church, 1 Cor. xi. 19; so sure there will be many offences in marriage; but, he saith, these are trials who have faith, these are but trials who are good husbands and who are good wives. His anger must be in such a mood as if he did chide with himself, and their strife as it were a sauce made of purpose to sharpen their love when it waxeth unpleasant; like Jonathan's arrows, which were not shot to hurt, but to give warning, 1 Sam. xx. 20. Knowing once a couple which were both choleric, and yet never fell out, I asked the man how they did order the matter that their infirmity did not make them discord? He answered me,

23

When her fit is upon her, I yield to her, as Abraham did to Sarah; and when my fit is upon me, she yields to me; and so we never strive together, but asunder. Methought it was a good example to commend unto all married folks.

His next duty to love, is a fruit of his love; that is, to let all things be common between them, which were private before. The man and wife are partners, like two oars in a boat; therefore he must divide offices, and affairs, and goods with her, causing her to be feared, and reverenced, and obeyed of her children and servants, like himself, for she is an under officer in his commonweal, and therefore she must be assisted and borne out like his deputy; as the prince standeth with his magistrates for his own quiet, because they are the legs which bear him up. To shew this community between husband and wife, he is to maintain her as he doth himself, because Christ saith, Mark x. 8, 'They are no more two, but one.' Therefore, when he maintaineth her, he must think it but one charge, because he maintaineth no more but himself, for they two are one. He may not say, as husbands are wont to say, that which is thine is mine, and that which is mine is mine own; but that which is mine is thine, and myself too. For as it is said, Rom. viii. 32, 'He which hath given us his Son, can he

24

deny us anything?' So she may say, He which hath given me himself, can he deny me anything? The body is better than the goods; therefore if the body be mine, the goods are mine too.

Lastly, he must tender her as much as all her friends, because he hath taken her from her friends, and covenanted to tender her for them all. To shew how he should tender her, Peter saith, 'Honour the woman as the weaker vessel,' 1 Peter iii. 7. As we do not handle glasses like pots, because they are weaker vessels, but touch them nicely and softly for fear of cracks, so a man must entreat his wife with gentleness and softness, not expecting that wisdom, nor that faith, nor that patience, nor that strength in the weaker vessel, which should be in the stronger; but think when he takes a wife he takes a vineyard, not grapes, but a vineyard to bear him grapes; therefore he must sow it, and dress it, and water it, and fence it, and think it a good vineyard, if at last it bring forth grapes. So he must not look to find a wife without a fault, but think that she is committed to him to reclaim her from her faults; for all are defective. And if he find the proverb true, that in space cometh grace, he must rejoice as much at his wife when she amendeth, as the husbandman rejoiceth when his vineyard beginneth to fructify.

25

Abraham said to Lot, 'Are we not brethren?'
Gen. xiii. 8, that is, may brethren jar? But they
may say, Are we not one? Can one chide with
another? Can one fight with another? He is a
bad host that welcomes his guest with stripes.
Doth a king trample his crown? Solomon calleth
the wife, 'the crown of her husband,' Prov. xii. 4;
therefore he which woundeth her, woundeth his
own honour. She is a free citizen in thine own
house, and hath taken the peace of thee the first
day of her marriage, to hold thy hand till she
release thee again.

Paul saith, Col. iii. 19, 'Be not bitter to your
wives,' noting, that anger in a husband is a vice.

Doth the cock spur the hen? Every man is
ashamed to lay his hands on a woman, because
she cannot match him; therefore he is a shame-
less man which layeth hands on his wife. The
hand doth not buffet its own cheek, but stroke it.
If a man be seen raging with himself, he is carried
to bedlam; so these madmen which beat themselves should be sent to bedlam till their madness
be gone. Solomon saith, Prov. v. 19, 'Delight
continually in her love,' that is, begin, proceed,
and end in love. In revenge, therefore, he sheweth
that delight is gone, because he calleth love their
delight. Thus we have sent letters unto husbands
to read before they fight. Now let us go home

26

to love again. Wouldst thou learn how to make thy match delightful? Solomon saith, 'rejoice in her love continually,' Prov. v. 19. As though thou couldst not delight without love, and with love thou mayest delight continually, therefore love is called the thankful virtue, because it rendereth peace, and ease, and comfort to them that make use of her. So much for husbands.

Likewise the woman may learn her duty of her names. They are called *goodwives*, as good-wife A and goodwife B. Every wife is called a good wife; therefore if they be not good wives, their names do belie them, and they are not worth their titles, but answer to a wrong name, as players do upon a stage. This name pleaseth them well. But besides this, a wife is called a yoke-fellow, to shew that she should help her husband to bear his yoke, that is, his grief must be her grief; and whether it be the yoke of poverty, or the yoke of envy, or the yoke of sickness, or the yoke of imprisonment, she must submit her neck to bear it patiently with him, or else she is not his yoke-fellow, but his yoke; as though she were inflicted upon him for a penalty, like to Job's wife, whom the devil left to torment him when he took away all he had beside.

Besides a yoke-fellow, she is called a helper, Gen. ii. 18, to help him in his business, to help him in his labours, to help him in his sickness, like a woman-physician, sometime with her strength, and sometime with her counsel.

Beside a helper, she is called a comforter too; and therefore the man is bid rejoice in his wife, Prov. v. 18; which is as much as to say, that wives must be the rejoicing of their husbands, even like David's harp to comfort Saul, 1 Sam. xvi. 23.

The daughters of Sarah are bound to call their husbands lords, as Sarah called her husband, Gen. xviii. 12, 1 Peter iii. 3, 6; that is, to take them for lords, for heads and governors. If ye disdain to follow Abraham's spouse, the apostle biddeth you follow Christ's spouse; for he saith, Eph. v. 24, 'Let a wife be subject to her husband, as the church is to Christ.' 'A greater love than this,' saith Christ, 'no man can have,' John xv. 13; so a better example than this no woman can have. That the wife may yield this reverence to her husband, Paul would have her attire to be modest and orderly, 1 Tim. ii. 9; for garish apparel hath taught many gossips to disdain their husbands. This is the folly of some men, to lay all their pride upon their wives; they care not how they sloven themselves, so their wives jet like peacocks. But Peter doth commend Sarah for her attire, and not Abraham, 1 Peter iii. 5,

shewing that women should brave it no more
than men; and God made Eve's coat of the
same cloth that he made Adam's, Gen. iii. 21.
They covered themselves with leaves, and God
derided them, Gen. iii. 7; but now they cover
themselves with pride, like Satan which is fallen
down before them like lightning, Luke x. 18.
Ruff upon ruff, lace upon lace, cut upon cut,
four-and-twenty orders, until the woman be not
so precious as her apparel; that if any man
would picture vanity, he must take a pattern of
a woman, or else he cannot draw her likeness.
As Herodias was worse for her fine dancing,
Mat. xiv. 6, so a woman may have too many
ornaments. Frizzled locks, naked breasts, paint-
ing, perfume, and especially a rolling eye, are the
forerunners of adultery; and he which hath such
a wife, hath a fine plague. Once women were
married without dowries, because they were well
nurtured; but now, if they weighed not more in
gold than in godliness, many should sit like nuns
without husbands. Thus we have shadowed the
man's duty to his wife, and the woman's to her
husband.

After their duties one to another, they must
learn their duties to their family. One compareth
the master of the house to the seraphin, which
came and kindled the prophet's zeal; so he should

go every day? Therefore Paul is so earnest with Philemon to make much of Onesimus his servant, that he desired Philemon to receive him as he would himself, Philem. 17. Therefore, because cruel and greedy masters should not use them too hardly, God remembered them in his creation, and made every week one day of rest, wherein they should be as free as their masters, Gen. ii. 2; so God pitieth the labourer from heaven, and every Sabbath looks down upon him from heaven, as if he should say, One day thy labours shall have an end, and thou shalt rest for ever, as thou restedst this day.

By this we see, as David did limit Joab, that he should not kill Absalom, 2 Sam. xviii. 5, so God hath bound masters, that they should not oppress their servants. Shall God respect thine more than thou? Art thou made fresher to thy labour by a little rest? And is not thy servant made stronger by rest to labour for thee? How many beasts and sheep did Laban lose, only for hardly entreating of a good servant, Gen. xxxi. 9; therefore that is the way to lose, but not to thrive.

Our Lord is called a servant, Isa. xlii. 1, Mat. xii. 18, which teacheth Christians to use their servants well for Christ's sake, seeing they are servants too, and have one master, Christ. As David speaketh of man, Ps. viii. 6, saying, 'thou hast made him a little lower than the angels,' so I may say of servants, that God hath made them a little lower than children; not children, but the next to children, as one would say, inferior children, or sons in law. And therefore the householder is called *pater familias*, which signifieth the father of his family, because he should have a fatherly care over his servants, as if they were his children, and not use them only for their labour, like beasts.

Lastly, we put the duty towards children, because they come last to their hands. In Latin, children are called *pignora*, that is, *pledges*; as if I should say, A pledge of the husband's love to the wife, and a pledge of the wife's love toward the husband; for there is nothing which doth so knit love between the man and the wife as the fruit of the womb. Therefore, when Leah began to conceive, she said, 'Now my husband will love me,' Gen. xxx. 20; as though the husband did love for children. If a woman have many defects (as Leah had), yet this is the amends which she makes her husband, to bring him children, which is the right wedding-ring, that sealeth and maketh up the marriage. When their father and mother fall out, they perk up between them like little mediators, and with many pretty sports make truce, when others dare not speak to them.

Therefore, now let us consider what these little ones may challenge of their parents, that stand them instead of lawyers. Before we teach parents to love their children, they had need be taught not to love them too much, for David's darling was David's traitor; and this is the manner of God, when a man begins to set anything in God's room, and love it above him which gave it, either to take away it, or to take away him, before he provoke him too much. Therefore, if parents would have their children live, they must take heed not to love them too much; for the giver is offended when the gift is more esteemed than he.

The first duty is the mother's, that is, to nurse her child at her own breasts, as Sarah did Isaac, Gen. xxi. 7; and therefore Isaiah joineth the nurse's name and the mother's name both in one, and calleth them 'nursing mothers'; shewing that mothers should be the nurses. So when God chose a nurse for Moses, Exod. ii. 8, he led the handmaid of Pharaoh's daughter to his mother, as though God would have none nurse him but his mother. After, when the Son of God was born, his Father thought none fit to be his nurse but the virgin his mother, Mat. ii. 14. The earth's fountains are made to give water, and the breasts of women are made to give suck. Every beast and every fowl is bred of the same

32

that did bear it, only women love to be mothers, but not nurses. Therefore, if their children prove unnatural, they may say, Thou followest thy mother, for she was unnatural first, in locking up her breasts from thee, and committing thee forth like a cuckoo, to be hatched in a sparrow's nest. Hereof it comes that we say, 'He sucked evil from the dug'; that is, as the nurse is affected in her body or in her mind, commonly the child draweth the like infirmity from her, as the eggs of a hen are altered under the hawk. Yet they which have no milk, can give no milk. But whose breasts have this perpetual drought? Forsooth, it is like the gout; no beggars may have it, but citizens or gentlewomen. In 1 Kings ii. 2, we have David instructing his sons; in Gen. xlix., Jacob correcting his sons; and in Job i., Job praying for his sons. These three put together,— instructing, correcting, and praying,—make good children, and happy parents.

Once Christ took a child, and set him in the midst of his disciples, and said, 'He which will receive the kingdom of heaven, must receive it as a little child,' Luke xviii. 17; shewing that our children should be so innocent, so humble, and so void of evil, that they may be taken for examples of the children of God. Therefore, in Ps. cxxvii. 3, children are called 'the heritage of the Lord,' to shew that they should be trained as though they were not men's children, but God's, that they may have God's heritage after. Thus if you do, your servants shall be God's servants, and your children shall be God's children, and your house shall be God's house, like a little church, when others are like a den of thieves, Col. iv. 15.

If thou hast read all this book, and art never the better, yet catch this flower before thou go out of the garden, and peradventure the scent thereof will bring thee back to smell the rest. As the corpse of Asahel made the passengers to stand, 2 Sam. ii. 23, so I placed this sentence in the door of thy passage, to make thee stand and consider what thou doest before thou marriest. For this is the scope and operation of it, to call thy mind to a solemn meditation, and warn thee to live in marriage as in a temptation, which is like to make him worse than he was, as the marriage of Jehoram did, 2 Chron. xxi. 6, if he use not Job's preservative, to be jealous over all his life, Job ix. 28.

The allurements of beauty, the troubles about riches, the charges of children, the losses by servants, the unquietness of neighbours, cry unto him that he is entered into the hardest vocation of all other; and therefore they which have but nine years' apprenticeship to make them good mercers or drapers, have nineteen years before marriage to learn to be good husbands and wives; as though it were a trade of nothing but mysteries, and had need of double time over all the rest.

Therefore, so often as you think upon this saying, think whether you be examples of it, and it will waken you, and chide you, and lead you a straight path, like the angel which led the servant of Abraham, Gen. xxiv. 40.

Thus have I chalked the way to prepare you unto marriage, as the Levites prepared their brethren to the passover, 2 Chron. xxxv. 6. Remember that this day you are made one, and therefore must have but one will. And now the Lord Jesus, in whom you are contracted, knit your hearts together, that ye may love one another like David and Jonathan, 1 Sam. xviii. 1; and go before you in this life like the star which went before the Gentiles, Mat. ii. 9, that ye may begin, and proceed, and end, in his glory! To whom be all glory for ever! Amen.

THE TRUE TRIAL OF THE SPIRITS

*Quench not the Spirit. Despise not prophesying.
Try all things, and keep that which is good.
Abstain from all appearance of evil.—*
1 Thes. v. 19–22.

AT the last time when I spake of these words,
'In all things give thanks,' and 'Quench not the
Spirit,' touching the first, I shewed you that it is
an easier thing to obtain of God than to be thankful to him; for more have gone away speeders
than have gone away thankers, Luke xvii. 17.

After speaking of those words, *Quench not the
Spirit*, I shewed you that the Spirit doth signify
the gifts and motions of the Spirit. The Spirit
in the 3rd of Matthew is likened to fire; and
therefore Paul saith well, 'Quench not the Spirit,'
because fire may be quenched.

Then I shewed you how the Spirit is quenched,
as a man doth quench his reason with over-much
wine; and therefore we say, When the wine is in,
the wit is out; because before, he seems to
have reason, and now he seems to have none;

36

so our zeal, and our faith, and our love, are quenched with sin. Every vain thought, and every idle word, and every wicked deed, is like so many drops to quench the Spirit of God. Some quench it with the business of this world ; some quench it with the lusts of the flesh ; some quench it with the cares of the mind ; some quench it with long delays, that is, not plying the motion when it cometh, but crossing the good thoughts with bad thoughts, and doing a thing when the Spirit saith, Do it not ; as Ahab went to battle after he was forbidden. Sometime a man shall feel himself stirred to a good work, as though he were led to it by the hand ; and again, he shall be frighted from some evil thing, as though he were reproved in his ear ; then, if he resist, he shall straight feel the Spirit going out of him, and hear a voice pronouncing him guilty, and he shall hardly recover his peace again. Therefore Paul saith, 'Grieve not the Spirit,' Eph. iv. 30 ; shewing that the Spirit is often grieved before it be quenched ; and that when a man begins to grieve, and check, and persecute the Spirit lightly, he never ceaseth until he have quenched it ; that is, until he seem to have no spirit at all, but walketh like a lump of flesh.

After *Quench not the Spirit*, followeth *Despise not prophesying*. In the end of this epistle, Paul speaketh like a father which is come to the end of his life; who, because he hath but a little while to speak, heapeth his lessons together, which he would have his sons remember when he is gone. So Paul, as though he were set to give good counsel, and had not leisure to speak that he would, sendeth the Thessalonians a brief of his mind, which their meditation should after amplify and expound unto them.

His first advice is, 'Quench not the Spirit'; that is, when a good motion cometh, welcome it like a friend, and cross it not with thy lusts. The second admonition teacheth how the first should be kept, 'Despise not prophesying'; and the Spirit will not quench, because prophesying doth kindle it. The third admonition teacheth how to make fruit of the second. Try the doctrines of them which prophesy, and thou shalt not believe error for truth, but hold the best. The fourth admonition is the sum of all, and it cometh last, because it is longest in learning; that is, 'Abstain from all appearance of evil.' This is the sum of all.

If you mark, Paul saith not, despise not *prophets*, but *prophesying*; signifying, that from the contempt of the prophets, at last we come to despise prophesying too, like the Jews, who, when they were offended with the prophet, charged him to prophesy no more, Jer. xi. 21. Therefore, as Christ warned his disciples to hear the Scribes and Pharisees, although they did not as they taught, Mat. xxiii. 3 ; so Paul warned the Thessalonians, that if any prophets among them do not as they teach, and therefore seem worthy to be despised, like the Scribes and Pharisees, yet that they take heed that they do not despise prophesying for the prophets. Because the preachers are despised before the word be despised, therefore we will speak first of their contempt.

Christ asked his disciples what they thought of him, Mat. xvi. 13, so I would ask you, what you think of preachers. Is he a contemptible person which bringeth the message of God, which hath the name of an angel, 2 Cor. v. 20, and all his words are messengers of life ? Prophets are of such account with God, that it is said, Amos iii. 7, 'God will do nothing before he reveals it unto his prophets'; so prophets are, as it were, God's counsellors. Again, kings, and priests, and prophets, were figures of Christ ; all these three were anointed with oil, to shew that they had greater graces than the rest ; but especially the prophets are called men of God, 1 Kings xiii. 1, to shew, that all which are of God will make much of prophets for God's sake. Therefore when the prophet Elisha would send for Naaman the leper to come unto him, these were his words, Naaman

'shall know that there is a prophet in Israel,'
2 Kings v. 8 : as though all the glory of Israel
were chiefly in this, that they had prophets, and
others had none ; as if one parish should triumph
over another, because they have a preacher, and
the other have none. Therefore when this prophet
was dead, Joash the king came unto his corpse,
and wept over his face, and cried, 'O my father,
my father ! the chariots of Israel, and the horse-
men of the same !' 2 Kings xiii. 14 ; shewing that
the chariots, and horses, and soldiers, do not so
safeguard a city, as the prophets which teach it,
and pray for it. Therefore when God would
mark the Israelites with a name of greatest
reproach, he calleth them a people which rebuke
their priests, as if he should say, usurpers of the
priest's office, for they rebuke their priests, which
are appointed to rebuke them.

As Paul sheweth the Thessalonians how the
preachers of the word should be honoured, so he
teacheth the Philippians how to honour their
teachers, saying, 'Receive him in the Lord with
great gladness, and make much of such,' Philip.
ii. 29; that is, shew yourselves so glad of him,
that he may be glad of you. Have you need to be
taught why Paul would have you make much of
such? Because they are like lamps, which consume themselves to give light to others, so they

40

consume themselves to give light to you; because they are like a hen, which clucketh her chickens together from the kite, so they cluck you together from the serpent; because they are like the shout which did beat down the walls of Jericho, Josh. vi. 20, so they beat down the walls of sin; because they are like the fiery pillar which went before the Israelites to the land of promise, so they go before you to the land of promise; because they are like good Andrew, which called his brother to see the Messias, John i. 41, so they call upon you to see the Messias; and therefore make much of such.

If we should make much of prophets, how much should we make of prophesying! If we should love our instructors, how much should we love instruction! Simeon keeping in the temple met with Christ, Luke ii. 28; so many hearing the word, have met with knowledge, have met with comfort, have met with peace, have met with salvation; but without the word never any was converted to God. Therefore, whensoever the word is preached, every one may say to himself, as the disciples said to the blind man, 'Be of good comfort, he calleth thee,' Mark x. 49; be of good comfort, the Lord calleth thee; but when the word is not preached, then every man may say to himself, Beware, the devil calleth thee. When

41

the prophets went from Jerusalem, the sword, and famine, and pestilence, and all the plagues of God rained upon them, even as fire came upon Sodom so soon as Lot was gone out, Gen. xix. 24; therefore what may those lands fear, which use their prophets as the Jews used those which were sent to them? Amos calleth it an evil time, wherein the prudent keep silence, chap. v. 13, therefore this is an evil time, wherein the prudent are silent. Once Paul said to Timothy, 'Let no man despise thy youth,' 1 Tim. iv. 12, shewing that preachers should not be despised for their youth; but now they despise the young prophets and the old too. How is the double honour turned to single honour! Nay, how is our honour turned to dishonour! 'If I be a master,' saith God, 'where is my fear?' Mal. i. 6; so, if we be prophets, where is our reverence? Doth not the contempt of the prophets cry unto God, as well as the blood of Abel? Gen. iv. 10. When the messengers which were sent unto the vineyard for fruit were beaten of them which should have laden them, then it is said that the lord of the vineyard waxed wroth, and said that he would let out the vineyard to others, which should yield him the fruits thereof, Mat. xxi. 43. The meaning hereof is this, that when the preachers and teachers which Christ sendeth to his church for fruits are abused and persecuted of them whom they call to the banquet, then he will remove their light and his gospel to others, which will yield him the fruits thereof.

Hath not this despising of the preachers almost made the preachers despise preaching? The people's neglect of the prophets hath made the prophets neglect prophesying. The non-resident keeps himself away, because he thinks the people like him better because he doth not trouble them; and the drone never studieth to preach, for he saith that an homily is better liked of than a sermon; and they which would study divinity above all, when they look upon our contempt, and beggary, and vexation, turn to law, to physic, to trades, or anything, rather than they will enter this contemptible calling. And is not the ark, then, ready to depart from Israel?

The second thing which makes prophets and prophesying despised, is the lewdness and negligence of them that are able to do well in their ministry, and yet do contrary. It is said of Hophni and Phinehas, that by their corrupt sacrificing they made the people abhor the sacrifice, 1 Sam. ii. 17; so many, by their slubbering of the word (for want of study and meditation), do make men think that there is no more wisdom in the word of God than they shew out of it; and

43

therefore they stay at home, and say, they know as much as the preacher can teach them.

There is a kind of preachers risen up but of late, which shroud and cover every rustical, and unsavoury, and childish, and absurd sermon, under the name of the simple kind of teaching, like the popish priests, which make ignorance the mother of devotion; but indeed, to preach simply is not to preach rudely, nor unlearnedly, nor confusedly, but to preach plainly and perspicuously, that the simplest man may understand what is taught, as if he did hear his name. Therefore, if you will know what makes many preachers preach so barely, and loosely, and simply, it is your own simplicity, which makes them think, that if they go on and say something, all is one, and no fault will be found, because you are not able to judge in or out; and so because they give no attendance to doctrine, as Paul teacheth them, 1 Tim. iv. 16, it is almost come to pass, that in a whole sermon the hearer cannot pick out one note more than he could gather himself. Wheat is good, but they which sell the refuse of wheat are reproved, Amos viii. 6; so preaching is good, but this refuse of preaching is but like swearing: for one takes the name of God in vain, and the other takes the word of God in vain. As every sound is not music, so every sermon is not preaching, but

44

worse than if we should read an homily. In Jer. xlviii. there is a curse upon them which do the business of the Lord negligently. If this curse do not touch them which do the chiefest business of the Lord negligently, truly I cannot tell whom the prophet meaneth. These would not have prophesying despised, and yet they make it despised themselves.

The last thing which makes prophets and prophesying despised is, the diversity of minds. While one holdeth one way, and another another way, some leave all, and will be of no religion, until both parties agree; as if a patient should pine himself, and eat no meat at all, because one physician saith that this meat will hurt him, and another saith that meat will hurt him. These are the three enemies which make us and our labours despised.

After *Despise not prophesying*, followeth *Try all things*, as if he should say, Despise not prophesying, but for all that try prophesying lest thou believe error for truth; for as among rulers there be bad rulers, so among prophets there be false prophets. The men of Berea would not receive Paul's doctrine before they had tried it; and how did they try it? It is said they searched the Scriptures. This is the way which Paul would teach you to try others, whereby he

45

was tried himself; whereby we may see that if you read the Scriptures you shall be able to try all doctrines: for the word of God is the touch-stone of everything, like the light which God made to behold all his creatures. A man trieth his horse, which must bear him, and shall he not try his faith which must save him?

Now, when we have tried by the word which is truth and which is error, what should we do then? 'Keep that which is best': that is, stay at the truth, as the wise men stayed when they came to Christ. We must keep and hold the truth, as a man grippeth a thing with both his hands; that is, defend it with thy tongue, maintain it with thy purse, further it with thy labour, in danger and trouble, and loss and displeasure, come life, come death; think, as Christ did seal the truth with his blood, so thou must seal it with thy blood, or else thou dost not keep it, but let it go. Well doth Paul put *try* before *choose*, for he which trieth may choose the best, but he which chooseth before he try, takes the worse sooner than the best, and therefore the pope's priests, because the people should take superstition before religion, will never let them have the touch-stone, but keep them from the Scripture, and lock it up in an unknown tongue, which they cannot skill of, lest they should try their doctrines, like the men of Berea, Acts xvii.,

46

making religion a craft, as men call their trades. Therefore, as Josiah rejoiced that the book of God was found again, so we may rejoice that the book of God is found again, for when the people might not read it, it was all one as if they had lost it.

After *Try all things* and *keep the best*, followeth *Abstain from all appearance of evil*; as if he should say, That is like to be best which is so far from evil that it hath not the appearance of evil; and that is like to be the truth, which is so far from error that it hath not the show of error; whereby he sheweth that nothing should be brought into the church, or added to our religion, but that which is undoubted truth, without suspicion of error. It is not enough to be persuaded of our faith, but we must be assured of it; for religion is not built upon doubts, but upon knowledge. Here we may marvel why Paul biddeth us abstain from all appearance of evil, because sin, and heresy, and superstition are hypocrites; that is, sin hath the appearance of virtue, and heresy hath the appearance of truth, and superstition hath the appearance of religion. But by this the apostle doth note that there is no sin, nor heresy, nor superstition, but, if the visor be taken away from it, it will appear to be a sin, and heresy, and superstition, though at the first sight the visor do make it seem none, because it covereth the evil,

47

like a painted sepulchre upon worms and rotten bones.

Hereby we are taught to judge of all things as they are, and not as they seem to be. As we draw aside the curtain before we behold the picture, so we must remove our prudence and all surmises, and then behold the thing naked as it is, if we will know it indeed.

A DISSUASION FROM PRIDE, AND AN EXHORTATION TO HUMILITY

God resisteth the proud, and giveth grace to the humble.—I Pet. v. 5.

SAINT PETER teaching every man his duty, how one should behave himself to another, exhorteth all men to be humble, and abstain from pride; as though humility were the bond of all duties, like a list, which holdeth men in a compass, and pride were the make-bait over all the world: to which Solomon giveth witness, Prov. xiii. 10, saying, 'Only by pride man maketh contention'; because pride maketh everyone think better of himself than of others, whereby he scorneth to give place to the other; and therefore, when neither party will yield, as Abraham did to Lot, Gen. xiii. 2, how should there be any peace? Thus pride doth break the peace, and humility doth set it again; therefore, to toll men from pride to humility, as it were from the concubine to the right wife, the apostle sheweth how God is affected to pride, and what mind he beareth to humility:

'God resisteth the proud, and giveth grace to the humble'; as if he should whisper men in the ears, and say, Take heed how you company with pride, or give entertainment to her, for she is not Cæsar's friend; the king counteth her his enemy, and all that take her part; she hath been suspected ever since the angels rebelled in heaven, and Adam sought to be equal with God, Gen. iii.; therefore, his majesty hath a stitch against her, as Solomon had to Shimei, I Kings ii. 36, and would not have her favourites come in his court unless they hold down their mace, stoop when they enter. But if you can get in with humility, and wear the colours of lowliness, then you may go boldly, and stand in the king's sight, and step to his chamber of presence, and put up your petitions, and come to honour. For humility is very gracious with him, and so near of his counsel, that as David and Solomon say, he committeth all his secrets to her, Prov. iii. 32, Ps. xxv.

Many sins are in this sinful world! and yet, as Solomon saith of the good wife, Prov. xxxi. 29, 'Many daughters have done virtuously, but thou surmountest them all.' So I may say of pride, many sins have done wickedly, but thou surmountest them all; for the wrathful man, the prodigal man, the lascivious man, the surfeiting man, the slothful man, is rather an enemy to him-

self than to God; the envious man, the covetous
man, the deceitful man, the ungrateful man, is
rather an enemy to men than to God; but the
proud man sets himself against God, because he
doth against his laws; he maketh himself equal
with God, because he doth all without God, and
craves no help of him; he exalteth himself above
God, because he will have his own will, though it
be contrary to God's will. As the humble man
saith, 'Not unto us, Lord, not unto us, but to thy
name give the glory,' Ps. cxv. 1 ; so the proud
man saith, Not unto him, not unto him, but unto
us give the glory.

Men will praise thee, not when thou reformest
thyself to God, but when thou dost form thyself to
thy lusts; that is, they which will be strutters shall
not want flatterers, which will praise everything
that they do, and everything that they speak, and
everything that they wear, and say it becomes
them well to wear long hair; that it becomes
them well to wear bellied doublets; that it becomes them well to jet in their going; that it
becomes them well to swear in their talking.
Now, when they hear men soothe them in their
follies, then, think they, we have nothing else to
commend us, if men will praise us; for our vanities we will have friends enow. So the humour
swelleth, and thinks with itself, if they will look

upon me when I do set but a stout face upon it,
how would they behold me if I were in apparel!
If they do so admire me in silks, how would they
cap me, and curtsey me, and worship me, if I were
in velvets! If I be so brave in plain velvet, what
if my velvet were pinked, or cut, or printed! So
they study for fashions, as lawyers do for delays,
and count that part naked which is not as gaudy
as the rest, till all their body be covered over with
pride, as their mind with folly. Therefore David
saith, Ps. lxxiii. 6, that pride is as a chain unto
them, that is, it goeth round about them like a
chain, and makes them think that all men love
them, and praise them, and admire them, and
worship them for their bravery. Therefore, as
Saul said to Samuel, ' Honour me before this
people,' so the proud man saith to his chain, and
his ruffs, and his pinks, and his cuts, Honour me
before this people. All that he speaketh, or doeth,
or weareth, is like Nebuchadnezzar's palace, which
he built for his honour, Dan. iv. This is their
work so soon as they rise, to put a pedlar's shop
upon their backs, and colour their faces, and prick
their ruffs, and frizzle their hair, and then their
day's work is done, as though their office were to
paint a fair image every morning, and at night to
blot it out again. From that day that pride is
born in the heart of man, as the false prophets

were schooled to speak as the king would have
them, so their eyes, and feet, and tongues are
bound to speak, and look, and walk, as the proud
heart doth prompt them. If God were in love
with fashions, he were never better served than in
this age ; for our world is like a pageant, where
every man's apparel is better than himself. Once
Christ said, that soft clothing is in king's courts,
Mat. xi. 8 ; but now it is crept into every house ;
then the rich glutton jetted in purple every day,
Luke xvi., but now the poor unthrift jets as brave
as the glutton, with so many circumstances about
him, that if ye could see how pride would walk
herself, if she did wear apparel, she would even go
like many in the streets, for she could not go
braver, nor look stouter, nor mince finer, nor set
on more laces, nor make larger cuts, nor carry
more trappings about her, than our ruffians and
wantons do at this day. How far are these
fashions altered from those leather coats which
God made in paradise! Gen. iii. 21. If their
bodies did change forms so often as their apparel
changeth fashions, they should have more shapes
than they have fingers and toes. As Jeroboam's
wife disguised herself that the prophet might not
know her, 1 Kings xiv. 2 ; so we may think that
they disguise themselves that God might not
know them ; nay, they disguise their bodies so,

53

till they know not themselves; for the servant
goeth like the master, the handmaid like her
mistress, the subject like the prince, as though he
had forgotten his calling, and mistook himself,
like a man in the dark, which puts on another
man's coat for his own, that is too wide, or too
side for his body; so their attires are so unfit for
their bodies, so unmeet for their calling, so contrary to nature, that I cannot call them fitter than
the monsters of apparel.

But for pride, noblemen would come to church
as well as the people; but for pride, gentles would
abide reproof as well as servants; but for pride,
thou wouldst forgive thy brother, and thy brother
would forgive thee, and the lawyers should have no
work. But when thou thinkest of these things,
pride comes in, and saith, Wilt thou go like a
haggler, wilt thou follow sermons, wilt thou take
the check, wilt thou put up wrong? What will
men say? That thou art a mome, and a coward,
and a fool, and no man will reverence thee, but
every man will contemn and abuse thee. Thus
men are fain to put on the livery of pride, as they
put on the liveries of noblemen, to shroud and
defend them from the contempt of the world.
Who hath not felt these counsels in his heart,
which would not believe that any pride was in him?
Yet as Absalom was a worse son than Adonijah,

54

because Adonijah rebelled against his brother, I Kings i. 5, but Absalom rebelled against his father, so pride hath worse children than vanity of apparel. Tyranny in princes, ambition in nobles, rebellion in subjects, disobedience in children, stubbornness in servants ; name pride, and thou hast named their mother; therefore shall not God resist pride? which hath sowed so many tares in his ground.

Absalom thought that rebellion would make him a king, 2 Sam. xv. 2 ; but God resisted his pride, and his rebellion hanged him on a tree. Nimrod thought that Babel should get him a name, Gen. xi. ; but God resisted his pride, and the name of his building was called *confusion* ever since. Nebuchadnezzar built his palace for his honour, Dan. iv. ; but God resisted his pride, and his palace spued him out when his servants remained in it. Shebna builded a sepulchre for his memorial, Isa. xxii. ; but God resisted his pride, and buried him in another country, where he had no sepulchre provided. Herod hoped when the people cried at his words, 'It is the voice of God,' that he should be worshipped ever after as God ; but God resisted his pride, and before he descended from his throne, the worms so defaced his pomp, that none which called him God would be like unto him. So when women take more pains to dress themselves than they do all the year after, and pay dearer to maintain one vice than they need to learn all virtues, they think to please men by it; but God resisteth their pride, and all that see them, though they cap and curtsey to them, yet they think worse of them, and think that they would not wear these signs of lightness and pride, unless they were light and proud indeed. Thus if their apparel condemn them before men, how will it condemn them before God! If sin did not blind them, would they so deceive themselves to take the contrary way, and think that should honour them which disgraceth others? But as Balaam was stopped and knew not who stopped him, Num. xxii., so they are resisted, and know not who resisteth them. Though they do all to please, yet they can please none: they please not God, for God resisteth them; they please not the humble, for the humble are contrary to them; they please not the proud, for the proud do envy them which strive to be as proud as they; they please not themselves, because they cannot be so proud and brave as they would be; only they content and please the devil, because their pride doth entitle him to them.

Thus much of God's battles against the proud. Here Peter leaveth the proud with this brand in their forehead, 'This is the man whom God resisteth'; then he turneth to the lowly, and comforteth them, 'but he giveth grace to the humble'; as if he should say, You are like John the beloved disciple, which leaned on Christ's bosom, John xiii. 23; though God resisteth the proud, yet he will not frown upon you, but when he resisteth them, he will give grace unto you; as if he should say, The proud are without grace, for God giveth not grace unto the proud, but to the humble, according to that of Isa. lxvi. 2, ' To him will I look, even to him that is poor, and of a contrite heart, and trembleth at my words'; therefore 'learn of me,' saith Christ, Mat xi., 'to be humble and meek,' as though the humble and meek were his scholars. Therefore God must needs love the humble, because they are like his Son. They shall have his best gifts, of which he saith, 2 Cor. xii. 9, 'my grace is sufficient'; as he should say, He which hath given you his grace, can he deny you anything? as Paul saith, 'he which hath given us his Son, will he not give us all things with him?' Therefore grace may be called the gift of gifts, because all gifts come with grace, as the court goeth with the queen. Therefore fear not to be humble, lest you be contemned; for all the promises of God are made to humility.

This is the ladder whereby we must ascend,

Gen. xxviii. 12. Pride did cast us down, and humility must raise us up. As the way to heaven is narrow, Mat. vii. 13, so the gate is low, and he had need to stoop which entereth in at it; therefore be not proud, lest God oppose himself against you; but be humble, and the grace of God belongeth to you. 'He resisteth the proud and giveth grace to the humble.' If thou disdain to learn humility of man, learn it of God, who humbled himself from heaven to earth, to exalt thee from earth to heaven, to which kingdom (when the proud shall be shut out) the Lord Jesus bring us for his mercy's sake!

THE YOUNG MAN'S TASK

Remember thy Creator in the days of thy
youth.—Eccles. xii. 1.

AMONG the rest, I may call this Scripture *The
young man's task*, wherein the wise man sheweth
when is the best time to sow the seed of virtue,
that it may bring forth the fruit of life, and make
a man always ready to die. Let him remember
his Creator in the days of his youth, and all his
life shall run in a line, the middle like the beginning, and the end like the middle; as the sun
setteth against the place where it rose.

After Solomon had described man, like Martha,
troubling and toiling herself about many things;
at last he bringeth him to that one thing necessary,
which Christ taught Mary, and shews him that if
he had begun there at first, he had found that
which he sought without trouble, and been
happier many years since than he is now.
Therefore to them which are young, Solomon
shews what advantage they have above the aged;

59

like a ship which seeing another ship sink before her, looks about her, pulls down her sail, turneth her course, and escapes the sands, which would swallow her, as they had done the other.

So they which are young need not try the snares and allurements of the world, or the issues and effects of sin, which old men have tried before them, but take the trial and experience of others, and go a nearer way to obtain their wished desires. That is this, saith Solomon: if thou wouldst have any settled peace or hearty joy in this vain or transitory world, which thou hast been seeking all the time since thou wert born, thou must 'remember thy Creator,' which did make thee, which hath elected thee, which hath redeemed thee, which daily preserveth thee, which will for ever glorify thee. And as the kind remembrance of a friend doth recreate the mind, so to think and meditate upon God will supply thy thoughts, dispel thy grief, and make thee cheerful, as the sight of the ark comforted David; for joy, and comfort, and pleasure is where God is, as light, and cheerfulness, and beauty is where the sun is. Now, if thou wouldst have this joy, and comfort, and pleasure to be long, and wouldst escape those thousand miseries, vexations, and vanities, which Solomon, by many weary and tedious trials, sought to make naked before thee, and yet held all but vanity when he had found the way, thou must 'remember thy Creator in the days of thy youth' at the first spring-time, and then thy happiness shall be as long as thy life, and all thy thoughts while thou remainest on earth a foretaste of the glory of heaven. This is the sum of Solomon's counsel.

'*Remember*, O young man, in thy youth.' No more *rejoice*, but *remember*. Solomon mocked before, and shewed what they *did* remember; here he shews what they *should* remember. Lest any libertine should misconstrue him, and say, Solomon taught to rejoice, Solomon gave us leave to sin, Solomon said, Do as ye list, for you are young men, and have a privilege to be lascivious and vain; he recants with a breath, and denies forthwith his word, even where he spake it.

What said I? 'Rejoice, O young man, in thy youth'? I would say, 'Remember, O young man, in thy youth.' So God mocks us while we sin, like Micaiah, which bid Ahab fight against Aram, and then forbade him again; so he bids them rejoice, and forbids them again. Rejoice not in thy youth, but repent in thy youth. One would think that Solomon should have given this memorandum rather to old men than to young men, Let them repent which look to die. Oh, saith Jeremiah, Lam. iii. 27, 'It is good for a man to bear the yoke in his youth.' If it be good to suffer in youth, it is better to learn in youth. Therefore, if David wished that his tongue might cleave to the roof of his mouth if he forgot Jerusalem, Ps. cxxxvii. 6, what are they worthy which forget God, the King of Jerusalem? Can a child forget his father? Is not God our Father? Therefore, who is too young to remember him, seeing the child doth know his father? As the deepest wounds had need to be first tented, so the unstablest minds have need to be first confirmed. In this extremity is youth, as Solomon shews them before he teacheth them; for in the last verse of the former chapter he calleth youth 'vanity,' as if he should speak all evil in a word, and say that youth is even the age of sin. Therefore, when he had shewed young men their folly under the name of vanity, like a good tutor he taketh them to school, and teacheth them their duty, 'Remember thy Creator,' as though all sin were the forgetfulness of God; and all our obedience came from this remembrance, that God created us after his own image, in righteousness and holiness, to serve him here for a while, and after to inherit the joys which he hath himself, which if we did remember, doubtless it would make us ashamed to think, and speak, and do as we are wont. For what man doth remember his Creator, or why he was created, while he sweareth and forsweareth, and maketh his trade of sin, as though there were no God to judge, nor hell to punish? This is because the remembrance of God, which would wake sinners, is so chased from men, for fear it should curb them of their pleasures, that they dare not think of them, but strive to serve him hereafter. So he stands as it were at the ladder foot and keeps us off with these weapons, that we cannot get upon the first staff, but one thought or other pulleth us back, when the foot is in the stirrup ready to ride away from all our sins at once. Thus we have long purposed to serve God, and every man thinketh that he should be served, but we cannot accord of the time when to begin: one saith, When I am rich ; another saith, When I am free; another saith, When I am settled; another saith, When I am old, then my pleasure will leave me, and I shall be fitter to fast and pray, and sequester myself, but now I shall be mocked if I be not like others. Thus, like bad borrowers, when our day is past already, we crave a longer, and a longer, and yet a longer, till we be arrested with death; so the prince of creatures dieth before he considered why he lived; for as no discipline is used where Christ's discipline is neglected, so no time is observed where God's time is omitted.

It is an old saying, Repentance is never too

late; but it is a true saying, Repentance is never too soon. Therefore, we are commanded to run that we may obtain, 1 Cor. ix. 24, which is the swiftest pace of man. The cherubims were pourtrayed with wings before the place where the Israelites prayed, Exod. xxv. 20, to shew how quickly they went about the Lord's business. The hound which runs but for the hare, girds forth so soon as he sees the hare start; the hawk which flieth but for the partridge, taketh her flight so soon as she spieth the partridge spring; so we should follow the word so soon as it speaketh, and come to our Master so soon as he calleth. For he which will not come when God calls, whatsoever he say, it is impossible that he should resolve to come hereafter; for he which is evil, how should he resolve to be good? Therefore now or never, now and ever, the tree which buddeth not in the spring is dead all the year. When a married man is first married, he may use the matter so to win his wife unto him, or estrange her heart for ever. When a pastor cometh first to a place, with a small matter he may make the simple people like him, or dislike him, so long as he stayeth; when the heir comes to his lands, lightly all his tenants begin to speak well of him, or evil of him; when a prince cometh to the crown, by the laws which he maketh first, the people guess how he will rule

64

ever after, and either dispose their hearts to love him, or wish his death.

And if we can say of others, when we see a graceless boy, Thou wilt prove a wagstring if thou live to be older; why should we, if we begin as ill as he, think that we shall be better and better, which judge that he will be worse and worse? As the arrow is directed at the first, so it flieth all the way, over or under, or beside, but it never findeth the mark, unless it be levelled right in the hand; so they which make an evil beginning, for-speak themselves at the first, and wander out all their race, because when they should have levelled their life, they took their aim amiss. Therefore happy are they which have their arrow in their hand, and day before them, for they need not wish to be young again. Now kill the serpent in the egg, for when he is a serpent he will kill thee; if thou canst not overcome sin in the infancy, before the root fasten, and the fence be made about it, how wilt thou struggle with the lion, when he useth his paws, and sin is become like an old man, so tough and froward, that he will not hear?

There was a pool in Jewry where the sick and leprous lay, John v. 2; for at one time of the day the angel came and stirred the water, and then he which stepped in first was healed of his disease. He which stepped in first was healed, saith John;

B.   65   5

none but he which stepped in first; so he which taketh time is sure, but he which foresloweth time oftener faileth than speedeth. For when golden opportunity is past, no time will fit for her. If Elias would be served before the widow, when she had but a little cruse of oil, which was not enough to serve herself, will God be served after Elias? Will God be served after thee? nay, after the flesh, and after the devil? There be not many Simeons, but many as old as Simeon, which never yet embraced Christ in their hearts. They thought to repent before they were so old, yet now they doat for age, they are not old enough to repent yet. Nay, I answer, many masters of Israel, mayors, aldermen, sheriffs, justices, bailiffs, constables, gentlemen, know no more what it is to be born again, than Nicodemus which came by night; line after line, sermon after sermon, and the blackmoor like himself. All their terms are vacations, all their religion promises, and all their promises hypocrisies. Instead of catechising their children, as Solomon teacheth them, they catechise them to hunt and hawk, to ride and vaunt, to ruffle and swear, to game and dance, as they were catechised themselves, lest the child should prove better than his father, and then he is qualified like a gentleman. Is this to seek the kingdom of heaven first, or last, or not at all? Woe to the security, woe

to the stubbornness, woe to the drowsiness of
this age. The thief cometh at midnight, and we
sleep till the dawning of the day ; we let in Satan
before we bid him avoid; we sell our birthright
before it come to our hands ; we seek for oil when
our lamps should burn; this day passeth like
yesterday, and to-morrow we shall spend like this
day. If youth had need of legs, age had need of
wings to fly unto God. But as Christ said, ' The
poor receive the gospel,' though the rich be more
bound ; so we may say, the young men receive the
gospel, though the old men have more cause.

The young men follow Christ, the young men
hear the word, the young men sanctify themselves,
the young men stand for the church, the young
men bear the heat of this day ; old Noah is drunk,
old Lot is sleepy, old Samson hath lost his strength.
Once the younger brother did steal the blessing
from the elder, and now he hath got it again, as
the malice of Esau shews, which persecutes him
for it. I speak it to their shame, they that wear
the furs and scarlets, as though they were all
wisdom, and gravity, and holiness, even to the
skirts, may say as Zedekiah said to Micaiah,
'When did the Spirit depart from me and go to
thee?' when did zeal depart from us and go to you?
They are so nouseled to the world, and acquainted
with sin, that it is too late now for the word to

speak unto them ; they may look upon the signs of wisdom, and gravity, and holiness when they see their long beards, and grey heads, and side gowns, and ask, Why is this bush hanged out, and no wine within? What marvel, then, if they be not reverenced, but mocked and pointed at, when Shem and Japhet had need to come again, and cover their nakedness? What a shame was it to the Israelites when Christ said by a Canaanite, ' I have not found so great faith in Israel' ! So what a shame is it to the elders, that Christ may say again, I have not found so great faith, nor knowledge, nor zeal in masters, and fathers, and rulers, as in servants and children, and apprentices; which made an old father of this city say, which now is with God, that if there were any good to be done in these days, it is the young men that must do it ; for the old men are out of date, their courage stoops like their shoulders, their zeal is withered like their brows, their faith staggereth like their feet, and their religion is dead before them.

THE TRIAL OF THE RIGHTEOUS

Many are the troubles of the righteous, but the Lord delivereth him out of them all.— Psalm xxxiv. 19.

THIS verse hath three parts, for here the *righteous* are the agents, their condition *troubles*, and the Lord their *deliverer*. So many things fall out contrary unto our minds every day, that he which wanteth patience in this world, is like a man which standeth trembling in the field without his armour, because every one can strike him, and he can strike none. So the least push of pain, or loss, or disgrace, doth trouble that man more which hath not the skill to suffer, than twenty trials can move him which is armed with patience, like a golden shield in his hand, to break the stroke of every cross, and save the heart though the body suffer ; for while the heart is whole, all is well. 'A sound spirit,' saith Solomon, 'will bear his infirmity, but a wounded spirit what can sustain?' Prov. xviii. 14. Therefore, as the lid is made to open and shut, to save the eye, so patience is set to keep the soul, and

save the heart whole, to cheer the body again.
Therefore if you mark, when you can go by an
offence, and take a little wrong and suffer trouble
quietly, you have a kind of peace and joy in your
heart, as if you have gotten a victory, and the
more your patience is, still the less your pain is.
For as a light burden, borne at the arm's end,
weigheth heavier by much, than a burden of
treble weight, if it be borne upon the shoulders,
which are made to bear; so if a man set im-
patience to bear his cross, which is not fit to
bear, it will grumble, and murmur, and start,
and shrink, and let the burden fall upon his
head, like a broken staff, which promiseth to
help him over the water, and leaveth him in the
ditch.   But if you put it to patience, and set her
to bear it, which is appointed to bear, she is like
the hearty spies that came from Canaan, and
said, 'It is nothing to overcome them,' Joshua ii.
So patience saith, It is nothing to bear, it is
nothing to fast, it is nothing to watch, it is
nothing to labour, it is nothing to be envied, it
is nothing to be backbited, it is nothing to be
imprisoned.   'In all these things,' saith Paul,
'we are more than conquerors,' Rom. viii. 37.

Patience hath a device to draw such a skin
over our sores that shall make our poverty seem
riches, our reproaches seem honour, our bondage

seem liberty, our labour seem rest, our sorrow seem joy, our pain seem ease, our sickness seem health, and all that hurt us rejoice us, until we say with David, 'Thy judgments are pleasant,' shewing that God's justice is as pleasant to the patient as his mercies to others. Therefore what a peacemaker were this in the commonwealth, if the magistrate had patience to bear his envy, if the preacher had patience to bear his study, if the creditor had patience to bear his losses, if the bondman had patience to bear his service, if the husbandman had patience to bear his labour, if the sick man had patience to bear his pain, if the poor man had patience to bear his wants. For want whereof many think themselves in hell, and say that no man's pain is like their pain, no man's wants like their wants, no man's foes like their foes, no man's wrongs like their wrongs, when they can scarce tell where their pain holds them. Therefore, albeit few can brook of humility, and charity, and meekness, and thankfulness, and temperance, and those severe virtues which pull from pleasure; yet every man doth wish for patience, like a physician, to ease his grief by all means that they can. So they which are wicked, although they cannot see the goodness of other virtues, yet can see the goodness of patience, and perceive when

they see a patient man and an impatient man
both sick of one disease, yet both are not troubled
alike, but that he which hath most patience hath
most ease, and he which is most impatient is
most tormented, like a fish which strives with the
hook.   Therefore even those which cannot suffer
that they might have rest, yet sing the patient
proverb, 'In sufferance is rest.'

'Many are the troubles of the righteous, but
the Lord delivereth him out of all.'   Here be the
two hands of God, like a wound and a plaster ; one
casteth down, and the other raiseth up.   It is
good for a man to know his troubles before they
come, because afflictions are lightened in the
expectation ; therefore, God saith of Paul, Acts
ix. 16, 'I will shew him how many things he
shall suffer for me.'   God dealeth plainly, and
tells us the worst first ; what we shall trust to, as
Christ told his disciples at the first, 'If ye will be
my disciples, ye must take up the cross,' Mat. xvi.
24 ; cold entertainment, to break their fast with
the rod ! Other feast makers, saith Christ, broach
the best wine first, but Christ keepeth the best
till the last, John ii. 10.   This is the manner of
God's proceedings, to send good after evil, as he
made light after darkness, Gen. i. 3 ; to turn
justice into mercy, as he turned water into wine,
John ii. ; for as the beasts must be killed before

72

they could be sacrificed, so men must be killed before they can be sacrificed; that is, the knife of correction must prune and dress them, and lop off their rotten twigs before they can bring forth fruit. These are the cords which bind the ram unto the altar, lest when he is brought thither he should run from thence again; this is the chariot which carrieth our thoughts to heaven, as it did Nebuchadnezzar's, and our assumption before our assumption. This is the hammer which squareth the rough stones till they be plain, and smooth, and fit for the temple; this is the first messenger which is sent to compel them to the banquet, which will not come when they are invited. Because we are naturally given to love the world more than is good for us, therefore God hath set an edge of bitterness upon us to make us loathe it.

The cross is one of our schoolmasters in this life, and the best wisdom is dearest bought. Prosperity seeketh for nothing, but necessity seeketh, and studieth, and laboureth, and prayeth for her wants. As the rod maketh the scholar to ply his book, so all our knowledge is beaten into us; some learn their goodness of poverty, some of sickness, some of troubles. Adversity is the fit time to learn the justice, mercy, power, and providence of God; a fit time to learn the patience, wisdom, faith, and obedience of man; a fit time to learn the subtilty, frailty, and misery of this world.

When God doth visit the wicked, his punishments are called plagues, and curses, and destructions; the plagues of Egypt, the curse of Cain, the destruction of Sodom. But when he doth visit the righteous, his punishments are called corrections, and chastisements, and rods, which proceed from a Father, not to destroy us, but to try us, and purge us, and instruct us; therefore, when we are afflicted, one saith, That God letteth us blood to save our lives, for our lives are rank, and must be lopped. And as Jacob was blessed and halted both at one time, so a man may be blessed and afflicted together. Afflictions do not hinder our happiness, but our happiness cometh by affliction, as Jacob's blessing came with halting. As Christ was no sooner born but Herod sought his life, Mat. ii., so the new man is no sooner born of the Spirit but the serpent is ready to devour him, his brethren to banish him, and hell to swallow him. In all the world he hath no friend but he which made the world. This is the state of the church militant; she is like the ark floating upon the waters, like a lily growing among thorns, like the bush which burned with fire, and was not consumed, Exod. iii. 2. So the city of God is always besieged, but never ruined. Christians and persecutions close together like Christ and his cross. As Christ was made to bear his own cross, Luke xxiii. 33, John xix. 17, so they are made to hold their cheeks to the nippers, their faces to be buffeted, their backs to be scourged, their eyes to be pulled out. Their peace is persecution, their rest labour, their riches poverty, their glory reproaches, their liberty imprisonment. Although they be the sons of God, the brethren of Christ, the only heirs of heaven, yet because they suffer their hell here, they must be content to be subject to their enemies, to be abjects to their kinsmen, to be hated of most, to be contemned of all, to be persecuted over the earth, a very haven and receptacle of troubles.

When David spake of troubles, he spake of troops, and heaps, and stars, and sands; and therefore he saith *many*, as though he were fain to lay them down in the gross sum, not reckon them. By 'many tribulations,' saith Paul, Acts xiv., but how many he could not number; for, except our sins, there is not such plenty of any thing in the world as there is of troubles which come from sin. As one heavy messenger came to Job after another, chap. i. 14–16, so now since we are not in paradise, but in the wilderness, we

75

must look for one trouble after another. Therefore afflictions are called waters, because as one wave falleth upon another, so one trouble falleth upon another, Ps. xlii. 7–9.

As a bear came to David after a lion, and a giant after a bear, 1 Sam. xvii. 34, and a king after a giant, and Philistines after the king, so when they have fought with poverty, they shall fight with envy; when they have fought with envy, they shall fight with infamy; when they have fought with infamy, they shall fight with sickness, like a labourer which is never out of work. Thus you see the righteous in troubles, like the Israelites in exile, Exod. iii. 10. Now the Lord cometh like Moses to deliver them. Adversity seeketh out the promise, the promise seeketh out faith, faith seeketh out prayer; then God heareth, and mercy answereth. All this while Christ seemeth to sleep, as he did in the ship; now he rebukes the winds and waves, Mat. viii. 26, and troubles fly before him like a troop of wolves before the shepherd.

This should content the righteous, to be delivered at last; as David, quieted himself, saying, Ps. xli. 11, 'By this I know the Lord favoureth me, because mine enemies do not triumph over me'; not because I have no enemies, or because I have no troubles which would overcome me.

Therefore when he wrote down *many troubles*, he blotted it (as it were) with his pen again, as a merchant razeth his book when the debt is discharged; and instead of *many troubles*, he putteth in, *the Lord delivereth*. Because he forgiveth all sins, he is said to deliver from all troubles; to shew that we have need of no Saviour, no helper, no comforter, but him.

The lawyer can deliver his client but from strife; the physician can deliver his patient but from sickness; the master can deliver his servant but from bondage; but 'The Lord,' saith David, 'delivereth out of all.' As when Moses came to deliver the Israelites, he would not leave an hoof behind him; so when the Lord cometh to deliver the righteous, he will not leave a trouble behind him. But even as they pray in Ps. xxv. 'Deliver Israel, O Lord, out of all his troubles'; so he will answer them, 'Be thou delivered out of all thy troubles'; that is, this, and this, and this (that trouble that thou thinkest intolerable, that trouble which thou thinkest incurable); the Almighty hath might against all. When Job is tried, not a sore shall stick upon him. Therefore, as Elisha feared not when he saw as many angels as enemies, 2 Kings vi.; so, when you see as many mercies as troubles, let the comfort satisfy you, which satisfied Paul, 'Fear not; for I am with thee,'

77

Acts xxvii. 24, thy pardon is coming; like the angel which stayed the sword over Isaac's head, Gen. xxii. Read on but a little further, and thou shalt hear the voice which proclaimed war proclaim peace; many troubles in the beginning of the verse, and no troubles in the end. What physician hath been here? The Lord, saith David. 'The Lord was in this place,' saith Jacob, 'and I knew it not,' Gen. xxviii. 16; so the Lord is in affliction, and men know it not. He which saith, I put away thine iniquities, Isa. xliii. 25, must say, I put away thine infirmities. For there is no Saviour but one; which saith to death, 'I will be thy death.' As the woman was sick until Christ came, Mat. ix. 19; so until the Lord come, there is nothing but trouble. Many troubles of the righteous, but one deliverer of the righteous; many terrors, but one comforter. Troubles come in an hundred ways, like water through a grate; but mercy entereth always at one door, like a pardon which cometh only from the prince. Therefore, saith God, 'In me is thy help,' Hosea xiii. 9. 'I create comfort,' Isa. lxv. Mark that he calleth himself a Creator of comfort; that is, as there is but one Creator, so there is but one comforter; and as he created all things of nothing, so he createth comfort of nothing; that is, when all comfort is worn out, and no seed of

78

joy left to raise up comfort again, then he bringeth comfort out of sorrow, as he brought water out of the rock, Exod. xvii. 6, 8, 14; that we may say, ' The finger of the Lord hath done this.'

Thus Moses describeth the journey of the righteous, as if they should go through the sea and wilderness, as the Israelites went to Canaan, Exod. xiii. 18. Look not for ease nor pleasure in your way, but for beasts, and serpents, and thieves; until you be past the wilderness, all is strait, and dark, and fearful; but as soon as you are through the narrow gate, all is large, and goodly and pleasant, as if you were in paradise. Seeing then your kingdom is not here, look not for a golden life in an iron world; but remember that Lazarus doth not mourn in heaven, though he suffered pains upon earth, Luke xvi.; but the glutton mourneth in hell, that stayed not for the pleasures of heaven. To which pleasures the Lord Jesus bring us, when this cloud of trouble is blown over us! Amen.

THE GODLY MAN'S REQUEST

Teach us, O Lord, to number our days, that we may apply our hearts to wisdom.—Ps. xc. 12.

FIVE things I note in these words: first, that death is the haven of every man; whether he sit in the throne, or keep in a cottage, at last he must knock at death's door, as all his fathers have done before him. Secondly, that man's time is set, and his bounds appointed, which he cannot pass, no more than the Egyptians could pass the sea; and therefore Moses saith, 'Teach us to number our days,' as though there were a number of our days. Thirdly, that our days are few, as though we were sent into this world but to see it; and therefore Moses, speaking of our life, speaks of days, not of years, nor of months, nor of weeks; but 'Teach us to number our days,' shewing that it is an easy thing ever for a man to number his days, they be so few. Fourthly, the aptness of man to forget death rather than anything else; and therefore Moses prayeth the Lord to teach him to number his days, as though they were still slipping out of his mind. Lastly, that to remember how short a time we have to live, will make us apply our hearts to that which is good.

The first point is, that as every one had a day to come into this world, so he shall have a day to go out of this world. When Moses had spoken of some which lived seven hundred years, and other which lived eight hundred years, and other which lived nine hundred years, shewing that some had a longer time, and some a shorter, yet he speaks this of all, *mortuus est* ; at last comes in *mortuus est*, that is, *he died*, which is the epitaph of every man. We are not lodged in a castle, but in an inn, where we are but guests, and therefore Peter calls us strangers, 1 Peter ii. 11. We are not citizens of the earth, but citizens of heaven, and therefore the apostle saith, 'We have here no abiding city, but we look for one to come,' Heb. xiii. 14. As Christ saith, 'My kingdom is not of this world,' John xviii. 36, so we may say, My dwelling is not in this world, but the soul soareth upward whence she came, and the body stoopeth downward whence it came ; as the tabernacles of the Jews were made to remove, so our tabernacles are made to remove. Every man is a tenant at will, and there is nothing sure in life but death. As he which wrote this is gone, so I which preach it, and you which hear it, one coming in, and one going out, is to all. Although this is daily seen, yet it had need be proved, nay, every man had need to die, to make him believe that he shall die.

Before sin nothing could change us; now everything doth change us; for when winter comes we are cold, when age comes we are withered, when sickness comes we are weak, to shew that when death comes we shall die. The clothes which we wear upon our backs, the sun which sets over our heads, the graves which lie under our feet, the meat which goes into our mouths, cry unto us that we shall wear, and fade, and die, like the fishes, and fowls, and beasts, which even now were living in their elements, and now are dead in our dishes. Every thing every day suffers some eclipse, and nothing stands at a stay, but one creature calls to another, Let us leave this world. Our fathers summoned us, and we shall summon our children to the grave; first we wax old, then we wax dry, then we wax weak, then we wax sick, and so we melt away by drops; at last, as we carried others, so others carry us unto the grave. This is the last bed which every man shall sleep in; we must return to our mother's womb. Therefore Jacob calleth his life but a pilgrimage; therefore Paul called his life but a race, 2 Tim. iv. 7; therefore

David calleth himself but a worm, Ps. xxii. 6. A pilgrimage hath an end, a race hath a stop, a worm is but trodden under foot, and dead straight; so in an hour we are, and are not. Here we are now, and anon we are separated; and to-morrow one sickeneth, and the next day another sickeneth; and all that be here never meet again. We may well be called earthen vessels, 2 Cor. iv. 7, for we are soon broken; a spider is able to choke us, a pin is able to kill us, all of us are born one way, and die a hundred ways. As Elijah stood at the door of the cave when God passed by, 1 Kings xix. 9, so we stand in the passages of this world, ready to go out whensoever God shall call. We lose first our infancy, and then our childhood, and then our youth; at last, as we came in the rooms of others, so others come into our rooms. If all our days were as long as the day of Joshua, when the sun stood still in the midst of heaven, Joshua x. 13, yet it will be night at last, and our sun shall set like others. It is not long that we grow, but when we begin to fall, we are like the ice which thaweth sooner than it froze: so these little worlds are destroyed first, and at last the great world shall be destroyed too; for all which was made for us shall perish with us. What do you learn when you think of this, but that which Moses saith, to apply your hearts to wisdom? Death cometh after life, and yet guides to the whole life, like the stern of a ship; but for death there would be no rule, but every man's lust should be his law; he is like a king, which frighteth afar off, though he defer his sessions, and stay the execution, yet the very fear that he will come makes the proudest peacock lay down his feathers and is like a damp which puts out the lights of pleasure.

David numbered his days by a measure : 'My life,' saith he, 'is like a span long,' Ps. xxxix. 5. When he measured his life, he took not a pole, or an ell, nor a yard to measure it by, but a short measure, his short span, ' My life is like a span long.' Thus you have learned to number your days, or rather the hours of your days. As some came into the vineyard in the morning, and some at noon, and some at night, so some go out of this vineyard in the morning, some at noon, and some at night. Some men's life hath nothing but a morning, some have a morning and noon ; he which liveth longest, liveth all the day, and therefore the youngest of all pray but for this day, and if he live till to-morrow, then he prayeth for that day, saying still, 'Give us *this day* our daily bread.' So that a pleasant life may be compared but to a glorious day, and a sorrowful life to a cloudy day, and a long life to a summer's

84

day, and a short life to a winter's day. How
comes it to pass, that when a man dies, all his
years seem but so many days, and before he
dies, all his days seem so many years? Job
speaketh of all alike, 'Man which is born of a
woman hath but a short time to live,' Job xiv. 1.
Jacob was one hundred and thirty years old, and
yet when he came before Pharaoh, he said, ' Few
and evil have my days been.' Though Pharaoh
did not speak of days, but asked him 'how old he
was,' yet he answered of days, to shew that not
only his years but his days were few. Our fathers,
marvelling to see how suddenly men are, and are
not, compared life to a dream in the night, to a
bubble in the water, to a ship on the sea, to an
arrow which never resteth till it fall, to a player
which speaketh his part upon the stage, and
straight he giveth place to another; to a man
which cometh to the market to buy one thing
and sell another, and then is gone home again ;
so the figure of this world passeth away. This is
our life ; while we enjoy it, we lose it.

Of all numbers we cannot skill to number our
days. We can number our sheep, and our oxen,
and our coin; but we think that our days are
infinite, and therefore we never go about to
number them. We can number other men's
days and years, and think they will die ere it

be long, if we see them sick, or sore, or cold; but we cannot number our own. When two ships meet on the sea, they which are in one ship think that the other ship doth sail exceeding fast, but that their ship goeth fair and softly, or rather standeth still, although in truth one ship saileth as fast as the other; so every man thinks that the others post, and run, and fly to the grave, but that himself standeth stock still, although indeed a year with him is no longer than it is with the others. Beside that, we are given to forget death, we strive to forget it, like them which say, 'We may not remember,' Amos vi. 10.

Two things I note in these words: first, that if we will find wisdom, we must apply our hearts to seek her; then, that the remembrance of death makes us apply our hearts unto it. Touching the first, Moses found some fault with himself, that for all that he had heard, and seen, and observed, and was counted wise, yet he was new to begin, and had not applied his heart to learn wisdom, like the wise man, which saith, 'I am more foolish than any man; I have not the wisdom of a man in me,' Prov. xxx. 2. So insatiable and covetous, as I may say, are the servants of God, the more wisdom, and faith, and zeal they have, the more they desire. Moses speaketh of wisdom as if it were physic, which

86

doth no good before it be applied; and the part
to apply it to is the heart, where all man's
affections are to love it and cherish it, like a
kind of hostess.   When the heart seeketh it
findeth, as though it were brought unto her, like
Abraham's ram.   Therefore God saith, 'They
shall seek me and find me, because they shall
seek me with their hearts,' Jer. xxix. 13, as
though they should not find him with all their
seeking unless they did seek him with their
heart.   Therefore the way to get wisdom is to
apply your hearts unto it, as if it were your
calling and living, to which you were bound
'prentices.   A man may apply his ears and his
eyes as many truants do to their books, and yet
never prove scholars; but from that day which a
man begins to apply his heart unto wisdom, he
learneth more in a month after than he did in a
year before, nay, than ever he did in his life.
Even as you see the wicked, because they apply
their hearts to wickedness, how fast they proceed,
how easily and how quickly they become perfect
swearers, expert drunkards, cunning deceivers, so
if ye could apply your hearts as thoroughly to
knowledge and goodness, you might become like
the apostle which teacheth you.   Therefore, when
Solomon sheweth men the way how to come by
wisdom, he speaks often of the heart, as 'Give

thine heart to wisdom,' 'let wisdom enter into
thine heart,' 'get wisdom,' 'keep wisdom,' 'embrace wisdom,' Prov. ii. 10, iv. 5, xiii. 8, as though
a man went a-wooing for wisdom. Wisdom is
like God's daughter, that he giveth to the man
that loveth her, and sueth for her, and meaneth
to set her at his heart. Thus we have learned
how to apply knowledge that it may do us good ;
not to our ears, like them which hear sermons
only, nor to our tongues, like them which make
table-talk of religion, but to our hearts, that we
may say with the virgin, ' My heart doth magnify
the Lord,' Luke i., and the heart will apply it to
the ear and to the tongue, as Christ saith, ' Out
of the abundance of the heart the mouth speaketh,'
Mat. xii. 34.

I can but teach you with words, as John
baptized with water. As Moses prayed the Lord
to teach him to number his days, so you must
pray the Lord to teach you to number your days.
And now I lead you to number your days. It
may be that thou hast but twenty years to serve
God; wilt thou not live twenty years like a
Christian, that thou mayest live a thousand years
like an angel ? It may be that thou hast but ten
years to serve him; wilt thou not serve ten years
for heaven, which wouldst serve twenty years for
a farm ? It may be that thou hast but five years

to serve God; wilt thou not spend five years well, to redeem all thy years for five? Yet God doth know whether many here have so long to repent for all the years which they have spent in sin. If thou wert born but to-day, thy journey is not an hundred years; if thou be a man, half thy time is spent already; if thou be an old man, then thou art drawing to thy inn, and thy race is but a breath; therefore, as Christ said unto his disciples when he found them sleeping, 'Could ye not watch one hour?' so I say to myself, and to you, Can we not pray? Can we not suffer a little while? He which is tired can crawl a little way, a little further, one step more for a kingdom. For this cause God would not have men know when they shall die, because they should make ready at all times, having no more certainty of one hour than another. Therefore our Saviour saith, 'Watch,' because you know not when the Lord will come to take you, or to judge you; 'Happy are they which hear the word and keep it.' Thus you see that death is the last upon earth, that the time of man is set, that his race is short, that he thinks not of it, that if he did remember it, it would make him apply his mind to good, as he doth to evil. And now I end as I began, 'The Lord teach us to number our days, that we may apply our hearts to wisdom.' Amen.

THE ART OF HEARING

Take heed how you hear.—Luke viii. 18.

THERE is no sentence in Scripture which the devil had rather you should not regard than this lesson of hearing; for if you take heed how you hear, you shall not only profit by this sermon, but every sermon after this shall leave such instruction, and peace, and comfort with you as you never thought the word contained for you; therefore no marvel if the tempter do trouble you when you should hear, as the fowls cumbered Abraham when he should offer sacrifice. First, he labours all that he can to stay us from hearing; to effect this, he keeps us at taverns, at plays, in our shops, and appoints us some other business at the same time, that when the bell calls to the sermon, we say, like the churlish guests, We cannot come, Mat. xxii. If he cannot stay us away with any business or exercise, then he casts fancies into our minds, and drowsiness into our heads, and sounds into our ears, and sets temptations before our eyes; that though we

hear, yet we should not mark, like the birds which
fly about the church. If he cannot stay our ears,
nor slack our attention as he would, then he
tickleth us to mislike something which was said,
and by that make us reject all the rest. If we
cannot mislike anything which is said, then he
infecteth us with some prejudice of the preacher;
he doth not as he teacheth, and therefore we less
regard what he saith. If there be no fault in the
man, nor in the doctrine, then, lest it would convert us, and reclaim us, he courseth all means to
keep us from the consideration of it, until we have
forgot it. To compass this, so soon as we have
heard, he takes us to dinner, or to company, or to
pastime, to remove our minds, that we should
think no more of it. If it stay in our thoughts,
and like us well, then he hath this trick; instead
of applying the doctrine, which we should follow,
he turns us to praise and extol the preacher. He
made an excellent sermon! he hath a notable
gift! I never heard any like him! He which
can say so, hath heard enough; this is the repetition which you make of our sermons when you
come home, and so to your business again till
the next sermon come; a breath goeth from us,
and a sound cometh to you, and so the matter is
ended. If all these comers hear in vain, and the
tempter be so busy to hinder this work more than

any other, Christ's warning may serve for you, as
well as his disciples, 'Take heed how you hear,'
Mark iv. 24. There is a hearing, and a preparative
before hearing, Eccles. v. 1; there is a praying,
and a preparative before praying; there is a
receiving, and a preparative before receiving,
1 Cor. xi. 28. As I called examination the forerunner, which prepareth the way to the receiver,
so I may call attention the forerunner, which prepareth the way to the preacher: like the plough,
which cutteth up the ground, that it may receive
the seed. As there is a foundation, upon which
the stones, and lime, and timber are laid, which
holdeth the building together; so, where this
foundation of hearing is laid, there the instructions, and lessons, and comforts do stay and are
remembered; but he which leaneth his ears on
his pillow, goeth home again like the child which
he leadeth in his hand, and scarce remembereth
the preacher's text. A divine tongue and a holy
ear make sweet music, but a deaf ear makes a
dumb tongue. There is nothing so easy as to
hear, and yet there is nothing so hard as to hear
well. The Jews did hear more than all the world
beside, yet because they took no heed to that
which they heard, therefore they crucified him
which came to save them, and became the
cursedest people upon the earth, which were

the blessedest nation before; therefore the A B C
of a Christian is to learn the art of hearing. We
care how we sow, lest our seed should be lost;
so let us care how we hear, lest God's seed be lost.

As children play the truants in the school, so
men play the truants in the church. How many
come to hear me, and yet, peradventure, some do
not hear, while I speak of hearing! One hath no
pitcher, another hath left his pitcher behind him,
another hath brought a broken pitcher which will
hold no water; therefore Christ calleth us fishers;
for as a fisher taketh but a few in respect of those
which go by, so we reform but a few in respect of
them which go as they came.

Now of Christ's hearers. We find in the
Gospel that Christ had four sorts of hearers;
while I count them to you, think of what sort
you are, for I doubt not but that there be here
of all sorts. Some heard him to wonder at him,
like Herod, which was moved with the fame that
went of him. Some came to hear, because they
would know all things, that they might be able
to talk of them. It seems that Judas was such a
scholar, for he had learned to preach, but not to
follow. Some came to cavil and to trip him in
his speeches; of these hearers were the scribes
and pharisees, which would make him an enemy
to Cæsar. Some were like to the good ground,

93

which came to know what they might do, and
how they should believe; like the humble scribe
which inquired the way to heaven.

Now to our hearers. As there were wise
virgins and foolish virgins, so there are wise
hearers and foolish hearers. Some are so nice
that they had rather pine than take their food
of any which is licensed by a bishop, as if Elias
should refuse his food because a raven brought it
to him, and not an angel; some come unto the
service to save forfeiture, and then they stay the
sermon for shame; some come because they
would not be counted atheists; some come
because they would avoid the name of papists;
some come to please their friends. One hath a
good man to his friend, and lest he should offend
him, he frequents the preachers, that his friend
may think well of him; some come with their
masters and mistresses for attendance; some
come with a fame; they have heard great speech
of the man, and therefore they will spend one
hour to hear him once, but to see whether it be
so as they say; some come because they be idle;
to pass the time they go to a sermon, lest they
should be weary of doing nothing; some come
with their fellows; one saith, Let us go to the
sermon; Content, saith he, and he goeth for
company; some hear the sound of a voice as

they pass by the church, and step in before they be aware; another hath some occasion of business, and he appoints his friends to meet him at such a sermon, as they do at Paul's. All these are accidental hearers, like children which sit in the market and neither buy nor sell. But as many foxes have been taken when they came to take, so they which come to spy, or wonder, or gaze, or scoff, have changed their minds before they went home, like one which finds when he doth not seek.

As ye come with divers motions, so ye hear in divers manners: one is like an Athenian, and he hearkeneth after news; if the preacher say anything of our armies beyond the sea, or council at home, or matters at court, that is his lure. Another is like the pharisee, and he watcheth if anything be said that may be wrested to be spoken against persons in high place, that he may play the devil in accusing of his brethren; let him write that in his tables too. Another smacks of eloquence, and he gapes for a phrase, that when he cometh to his ordinary he may have one figure more to grace and worship his tale. Another is malcontent, and he never pricketh up his ears till the preacher come to gird against some whom he spiteth, and when the sermon is done, he remembereth nothing

95

which was said to him, but that which was spoken against others. Another cometh to gaze about the church; he hath an evil eye, which is still looking upon that from which Job did avert his eye. Another cometh to muse; so soon as he is set, he falleth into a brown study; sometimes his mind runs on his market, sometimes on his journey, sometimes of his suit, sometimes of his dinner, sometimes of his sport after dinner, and the sermon is done before the man thinks where he is. Another cometh to hear, but so soon as the preacher hath said his prayer, he falls fast asleep, as though he had been brought in for a corpse, and the preacher should preach at his funeral.

This is the generation of hearers. Is not the saying of Christ fulfilled now, 'Hearing you hear not'? because we hear and hear not; like a covetous churl which goeth by a beggar when he crieth in Christ's name for relief, and heareth him cry, but will not hear him, because he craveth that which he will not part with. May we not say again with Christ, 'What went ye out to see,' rather than, 'What went ye out to hear?' seeing ye remember that which ye see, and forget all that which ye hear. So you depart from our sermons like a slide-thrift's purse, which will hold no money.

THE ART OF HEARING

One thing is necessary, and all unnecessaries are preferred before it. The greatest treasure in the world is most despised, the star which should lead us to Christ, the ladder which should mount us to heaven, the water that should cleanse our leprosy, the manna that should refresh our hunger, and the book that we should meditate on day and night, Ps. i. 2, lieth in our windows, no man readeth it, no man regardeth it; the love of God, and the love of knowledge, and the love of salvation is so cold, that we will not read over one book for it, for all we spend so many idle times while we live.

This age hath devised divers methods to learn many things in shorter time than they were learned of old. A man may spend seven years in learning to write, and he may meet with a scribe which will teach him as much in a month. A prentice may spend nine years in learning a trade, and some master (if he were disposed), would teach him as much in a twelvemonth. A man may fetch such a compass that he may be a whole month in going to Berwick; and another, which knoweth the way, will go it in less than a week; so to every thing there is a further way, and a nearer way, and so there is to knowledge. You do not remember the hundredth part of that which you have heard, and to-morrow you will

not remember the tenth note which you have
heard this day. It may be that some will remember more; and why not thou as well as he?
because one useth an help of his memory, which
the other useth not. If you will use his policy,
you shall remember as well as he; for let him
neglect his help, and the best memory here shall
not carry away half which he marketh now, until
it be night. When the woman of Samaria heard
Christ speak of a water, of which 'he that drinketh
shall thirst no more,' Oh (saith she), 'give me of
that water.' So, now you hear of such a way,
you would fain know it, but will you use it? I
wish that I were such a messenger, that I could
compel you unto it; for truly until you use it,
you shall never learn faster than you do. Now I
think you have a desire to hear it, I will shew it
unto you; first, in mine opinion two things out of
every sermon are especially to be noted; that
which thou didst not know before, and that which
speaketh to thine own sin; for so thou shalt increase thy knowledge, and lessen thy vices.

Now if thou wouldest remember both these a
year hence as fresh as now, this is the best policy
that ever thou shalt learn, to put them presently
in practice; that is, to send them abroad to all
the parts of thy soul and members of thy body,
and reform thyself semblably to them, and thou

98

shalt never forget them, for thy practice remembereth them. But before this you must use another help, that is, record every note in thy mind, as the preacher goeth; and after, before thou dost eat, or drink, or talk, or do anything else, repeat all to thyself. I do know some in the university, which did never hear good sermon but as soon as they were gone they rehearsed it thus, and learned more by this (as they said) than by their reading and study; for recording that which they had heard when it was fresh, they could remember all, and hereby got a better facility in preaching than they could learn in books. The like profit I remember I gained, when I was a scholar, by the like practice.

What a shame is this, to remember every clause in your lease, and every point in your father's will; nay, to remember an old tale so long as you live, though it be long since you heard it; and the lessons which ye hear now will be gone within this hour, that you may ask, What hath stolen my sermon from me? Therefore, that you may not hear us in vain, as you have heard others, my exhortation to you is, to record when you are gone that which you have heard. If I could teach you a better way, I would; but Christ's disciples used this way

when their thoughts ran upon his speech, and
made them come again to him to ask the meaning ; the virgin his mother used this way when
she pondered his sayings, and laid them up in
her heart ; the good hearers of Berea used this
way, when they carried Paul's sermon home
with them, that they might examine it by the
Scripture.

If you will know why many preachers preach
so barely, loosely, and simply, it is your own
simplicity which makes them think that if they
go on and say something, all is one, and no
fault will be found ; because you are not able to
judge in or out ; and so because they give no
attendance to doctrine, as Paul teacheth them, it
is almost come to pass, that in a whole sermon,
the hearer cannot pick out one note more than
he could gather himself ; and many loathe
preaching, as the Jews abhorred the sacrifice for
the slubbering priests, which cared not what they
offered ; and the greater sort imagine that there
is no more wisdom in the word of God, than their
teachers shew out of it. What a shame is this,
that the preachers should make preaching be
despised ! In Jeremiah xlviii., there is a curse
upon them which do the business of the Lord
negligently ; if this curse do not touch them
which do the chiefest business of the Lord

negligently, it cannot take hold of any other. Therefore let every preacher first see how his notes do move himself, and then he shall have comfort to deliver them to others, like an experienced medicine, which himself hath proved.

THE MAGISTRATES' SCRIPTURE

*I have said, Ye are gods; and ye are all the
children of the Most High: but ye shall die as
a man, and ye princes shall die like others.—*
Ps. lxxxii. 6, 7.

I MAY call this text, *the Magistrates' Scripture*;
considering the state of kings and governors,
how much good they might do, and how little
they perform, God becomes a remembrancer
unto them. And first, shews what a high calling
princes and rulers have, and then, lest they
should be proud of it, and make their magistracy
a chair of ease, he turns upon them again, as
though he had another message unto them, and
tells them, that though they be above others, yet
they shall die like others; and though they
judge here, yet they shall be judged hereafter,
and give account of their stewardship, how they
have governed, and straightway their subjects,
how they have obeyed. A good memorandum
for all in authority, so to deal in this kingdom,
that they lose not the kingdom to come.

I have said, Ye are gods, &c. How can he
call them gods, which calls himself the only God?
and saith, There are no more gods but he, Isa.
xliv. 6, xlv. 21. 'I have made thee Pharaoh's
god,' saith God to Moses, Exod. vii. 1, because
he had given him power to speak unto Pharaoh
in his name, and to execute his judgments upon
him ; so he calleth magistrates gods, because he
hath given them power to speak to the people
in his name, and to execute his judgments upon
them. Out of this name rulers may learn how
to govern, and subjects how to obey. As the
inferior magistrates do nothing but as the
superior magistrate prescribeth, so they which
rule under God, for God, must rule by the pre-
script of God, and do nothing but as their conscience tells them that God would do himself.
Therefore they which use their power against
God, which bear the person of God and execute
the will of the devil, which make laws against
God's law, and be enemies to his servants, are
worse than Balaam, which would not curse whom
God blessed, Num. xxii. 18 ; and so much as in
them lieth, make God a liar, because they cannot
so well be called gods, as devils. Such gods go
to hell.

This extolleth the calling of magistrates. As
Jacob honoured Joseph's children, when he said

they should be called after his name, Gen. xlviii.
16 ; so God honoureth the magistrates when he
gives them his own name, calling them gods, as
though they were a kind of godhead in them.
'These things pertain to the wise,' Prov. xxiv. 23,
and they themselves do not always see it ; yet he
which hath a spiritual eye, and carries the pattern
of God in his heart, may see another likeness of
God in magistrates, than in common persons.
As the builders of the temple had a special
wisdom and spirit, which God gave them for that
work which they were chosen to, Exod. xxxi. 3
and xxxv. 31, so when Samuel had anointed
David, he saith, that 'the Spirit of the Lord
came upon David from that day forward,' 1 Sam.
xvi. 13, as though he had another spirit after than
he had before.   There is a difference between
kings and inferior magistrates ; for the prince is
like a great image of God, the magistrates are
like little images of God, appointed to rule for
God, to make laws for God, to reward for God,
to punish for God, to speak for God, to fight for
God, to reform for God, and therefore their
battles are called 'The Lord's battles' ; and their
judgments, 'The Lord's judgments' ; and their
throne, 'The Lord's throne' ; and the kings
themselves, 'His kings,' to shew that they are all
for God, like his hands. By some he teacheth

mercy, by some justice, by some peace, by some
counsel, as Christ distributed the loaves and
the fishes by the hands of his disciples, Mat. xiv.
18. This God requires of all when he calls them
gods, to rule as he would rule, judge as he would
judge, correct as he would correct, reward as he
would reward, because it is said, that they are
instead of the Lord God ; that is, to do as he
would do, as a scholar writes by a copy. This
is a good study for magistrates in all their
judgments, to consider what God would do,
because they are instead of God, I rule for God,
I speak for God, I judge for God, I reward for
God, I correct for God ; then as he would do and
determine, so must be my sentence.

They are called gods, to encourage them in
their office, and to teach them that they need
not dread the persons of men ; but as God doth
that which is just and good without the jealousy
of men, so they, upon the bench, and in all
causes of justice, should forget themselves to be
men, which are led by the arms between favour
and fear, and think themselves gods, which fear
nothing. This boldness is so necessary in them
which should judge all alike.

This is the religion of these times : they fear
nothing more than to be counted too precise ;
but God doth call them more than precise, for he

calls them gods ; of all men they should not
forget his name. Princes and rulers have many
names of honour, but this is the honourablest
name in their titles, that they are called gods ;
other names have been given them of men for
reverence, or flattery, but no man could give
them this name but God himself. Therefore
their name is a glass wherein they may see their
duty.

Thus their name tells them how they should
rule, and by consequence teacheth how we
should obey. God calls them gods, therefore he
which contemneth them, contemneth God ; God
calls them fathers, therefore we must reverence
them like fathers ; God calls them kings, princes,
lords, judges, powers, rulers, governors, which
are names of honour ; and shall we dishonour
them whom God doth honour? Our first lesson
is, 'Fear God'; the next is, 'Honour the king,'
Prov. xxiv. 21, 1 Peter ii. 17 ; that is (as Paul
interpreteth), we must 'obey for conscience,'
Rom. xiii. 5, not against conscience ; for that
were to put a stranger before the king, and the
king before God, which, Christ saith, have no
power but from God, John xix. 11 ; and therefore
cannot make themselves magistrates, Heb. v. 4,
no more than they can make themselves gods.
As none could give this name but God, so no

man which exalteth himself can challenge this
honour, no more.

It followeth, *but ye shall die as a man.* Here
he distinguisheth between mortal gods and the
immortal God. Ye have seen their glory; now
behold their end, 'They shall all die like others.'
Though they be never so rich, so goodly, so
mighty, so honourable while their date lasteth,
yet they may as truly as Job call 'corruption their
father, and the worm their mother,' Job xvii. 14 ;
for the grave shall be the last bed of all flesh.
As they were born like men, so they shall die like
men ; the same coming in and going out is to
all. When Isaiah had said that 'all flesh was
grass,' as though he would correct his speech, he
adds, 'and the glory of it is as the flower of the
field,' Isa. xl. As if he should say, Some men have
more glory than others, and they are like flowers ;
the others are like grass : no great difference, the
flower shews fairer, but grass stands longer ; one
scythe cuts both down, like the fat sheep and the
lean, that feed in two pastures, but are killed in
one slaughter. So, though the great man live in
his palace, and the poor man dwells in his cottage,
yet both shall meet at the grave, and vanish
together. Even they which are lords, and judges,
and counsellors now, are but successors to them
which are dead, and are nearer to death now than

when I began to preach of this theme. It had been a great sessions for all others to die; but for magistrates, princes, for kings, for emperors to die as they die, what a battle is this that leaves no man alive! Shall the gods die too? He gives them their title, but he tells them their lot. Though their power, though their wealth, though their honour, though their titles, though their train, though their friends, though their ease, though their pleasures, though their diet, though their clothing be not like others', yet their end shall be like others', 'I have said that ye are gods, but ye shall die like other men.' But for this *die*, many would live a merry life, and feast, and sport, and let the world slide; but the remembrance of death is like a damp, which puts out all the lights of pleasure, and makes him rub, and frown, and whine which thinks upon it, as if a mote were in his eye. Oh how heavy tidings is this to hear thou shalt die, from him which hath life and death in his own hands, when the message is sent to them which reigned like gods! as if he should say, Even you which glister like angels, whom all the world admires, and sues and bows to, which are called honourable, mighty and gracious lords, I will tell you to what your honour shall come: first, ye shall wax old like others, then ye shall fall sick like others, then ye shall die like others, then ye shall be buried like others, then ye shall be consumed like others, then ye shall be judged like others, even like the beggars which cry at your gates : one sickens, the other sickens ; one dies, the other dies ; one rots, the other rots : look in the grave, and shew me which was Dives and which was Lazarus. This is some comfort to the poor, that once he shall be like the rich ; one day he shall be as wealthy, as mighty, and as glorious as a king ; one hour of death will make all alike ; they which crowed over others, and looked down upon them like oaks, others shall walk upon them like worms, and they shall be gone as if they had never been.

Where are they which founded this goodly city, which possessed these fair houses, and walked these pleasant fields, which erected these stately temples, which kneeled in these seats, which preached out of this place but thirty years ago? Is not earth turned to earth? and shall not our sun set like theirs when the night comes? Yet we cannot believe that death will find out us, as he hath found out them; though all men die, yet every man dreams, I shall escape ; or at the least, I shall live till I be old. This is strange, men cannot think that God will do again that which he doth daily, or that he will deal with them as he deals with others. Tell one of us that all others shall

die, we believe it ; tell one of us we shall die, and
we believe it sooner of all than of one ; though we
be sore, though we be weak, though we be sick,
though we be elder than those whom we follow to
the ground. So they thought which lie in this
mould under your feet, as you do. If wisdom, or
riches, or favour, could have entreated death,
those which have lived before us would have kept
our possessions from us ; but death would take no
bail, we are all tenants at will, and we must leave
this cottage whensoever the landlord will put
another in our room, at a year's, at a month's, at a
week's, at a day's, at an hour's warning, or less.
The clothes which we wear upon our backs, the
graves which are under our feet, the sun which sets
over our heads, and the meats which go into our
mouths, do cry unto us that we shall wear, and
set, and die like the beasts, and fowls, and fishes,
which now are dead in our dishes, and but even
now were living in the elements. Our fathers
have summoned us, and we must summon our
children, to the grave. Every thing every day
suffers some eclipse, nothing standing at a stay ;
but one creature calls to another, Let us leave
this world. While we play our pageants upon
this stage of short continuance, every man hath a
part, some longer, and some shorter ; and while
the actors are at it, suddenly death steps upon

the stage, like a hawk which separates one of the doves from the flight ; he shoots his dart ; where it lights, there falls one of the actors dead before them, and makes all the rest aghast ; they muse, and mourn, and bury him, and then to the sport again ! While they sing, play, and dance, death comes again and strikes another; there he lies, they mourn for him, and bury him as they did the former, and play again. So one after another till the players be vanished, like the accusers which came before Christ, John viii. 9 ; and death is the last upon the stage, so 'the figure of this world passeth away.' Many which stand here, may lie here or elsewhere within this twelvemonth. But thou thinkest it is not I, and he thinketh it is not he ; but he which thinks so cometh soonest to it. If I could make you believe that you have but a year to live, and that all which hear me this day shall come to the bar before this day twelve-month return again, ye would prepare yourselves to die, and leave your sins behind you, and depart Christians out of the church, with a mind to do all that God would have you. Thus I have pro-claimed to all kings, princes, judges, councillors, and magistrates, that which Isaiah foretold to one, ' Set thy things in order, for thou shalt die.'

THE LADDER OF PEACE

*Rejoice evermore.   Pray continually.   In all
things give thanks.*—1 Thes. v. 16–18.

WHEN I spake last of these words, I shewed
you how the apostle commendeth unto us three
virtues, of greater price than the three presents
which the wise men brought unto Christ : the
first is, ' Rejoice evermore '; the second is, ' Pray
continually '; the third, ' In all things give thanks.'
All three are of one last, for we must rejoice
continually, because he saith, Rejoice evermore ;
and we must pray continually, because he saith,
Pray continually ; and we must give thanks
continually, because he saith, In all things give
thanks.   These are the three things which, one
saith, all men do, and no man doth, because every
man doth them, and scarce one doth them as he
should ; therefore the apostle, to shew us how we
should do them well, doth put *continually* unto
them, as though continuance were the perfection
of all virtues.   I chose this scripture for a consolation to them which are afflicted in conscience,

which is commonly the disease of the innocentest soul, for they think that they do well to *mourn continually* ; and Paul saith, *Rejoice continually* ; and therefore I will speak a little more of these words than I did before. If you mark it, it may well be called *The Ladder of Peace*, for it stands upon three steps, and every step is a step from trouble to peace, from sorrow to joy ; for he which can rejoice, is past grief ; and he which can pray, is passing from his grief ; and he which can give thanks, hath obtained his desire. A man cannot rejoice and mourn ; a man cannot pray and despair ; a man cannot give thanks and be offended ; therefore keep still upon one of these three steps, and you shall never sorrow too much. If thou canst not rejoice, as if thy pain were past, then give thanks, because thy pain is profitable. If thou canst not think that thy pain is worth thanks, then pray that thou mayest have patience to bear it ; and it is impossible in praying, or thanking, or rejoicing, that any grief should want patience enough to bear it. But when you forget to rejoice in the Lord, then you begin to muse, and after to fear, and after to distrust, and at last to despair, and then every thought seems to be a sin against the Holy Ghost.

The Son of God is called, 'The consolation of Israel,' Luke ii. 25, to shew that he brings

THE SERMONS OF HENRY SMITH

consolation with him, and that joy is where
Christ is, as light is where the sun is; therefore
the chiefest joy is called 'The joy of the Holy
Ghost,' Rom. xiv. 17, to shew that they have
the chiefest joy which have the Holy Ghost;
therefore the greatest peace is called 'The peace
of conscience,' Philip. iv. 7, to shew that they
have the greatest peace which have a good conscience; therefore the faithful are said to be
'anointed with the oil of joy,' Isa. lxi. 3, as though
joy were in their countenance; therefore they are
said to be 'clothed with the garment of gladness,'
as though gladness did compass them like a
garment; therefore Paul, in all his epistles, doth
join 'grace and peace' together, Rom. i. 7, 1 Cor.
i. 3, 2 Cor. i. 2, Gal. i. 3, Eph. i. 2, Col. i. 2,
2 Thes. i. 2, Titus i. 4, Philem. 3, and shew that
the peace of God doth follow them which have
the grace of God. It is not in vain that the Holy
Ghost, when he named Barnabas, interpreted his
name too, because it signifieth 'the son of consolation,' Acts iv. 36; as though he delighted
in such men as were the sons of consolation.
'Comfort one another,' saith Paul, 1 Thes. iv. 18.
How shall we comfort one another without comfort? Therefore Paul saith, 'God comforteth us,
that we may be able to comfort others, by the
comfort whereby we ourselves are comforted of

114

God,' 2 Cor. i. 4, shewing that we cannot comfort
others unless we be comfortable ourselves ; and
therefore, that we may perform this duty, we are
bound to nourish comfort in ourselves. Paul saith,
' I am full of comfort,' 2 Cor. vii. 4 ; who then can
say, I am full of sorrow, but he must contrary
Paul ? As the body may not offend the soul, so
the soul may not injure the body, because it is
the body's keeper ; but a pensive man doth injure
the body and the soul too ; for Solomon saith,
'A sound spirit will bear his infirmities, but a
wounded spirit who can bear ?' Prov. xviii. 14 :
as if he should say, The heart must be kept
courageous, and strong, and lively, like an instrument which is tuned to tune all the rest, or else
every grief will make thee impatient. In Deut.
xxx. 9 it is said, that God 'rejoiceth to do us
good' ; and therefore, in Deut. xxviii., the Jews
are reproved, because they rejoiced not in the
service of God. As he loveth a cheerful giver,
so he loveth a cheerful server, and a cheerful
preacher, and a cheerful hearer, and a cheerful
worshipper ; and therefore David saith, ' Let us
sing heartily unto the Lord,' Ps. xcv. 1 ; shewing,
as it were, the tune which delighteth God's ears.
Therefore, let us pray God every day to turn all
our joy into the joy of the Holy Ghost, and all
our peace into the peace of conscience, and all

our sorrow into the sorrow for sin, and all our fear into the fear to sin, that so we may sorrow and rejoice together, fear and hope together ; that is, have one eye to the law, to keep us from presumption, and another eye to the gospel, to keep us from despair ; and then this comfort is sent to us, ' Rejoice evermore,' or else we have nothing to do with it.

Secondly, It is such a pleasant thing, that Paul joineth *pray continually* with *rejoice continually*, to shew that no man hath such joy, as he which is often talking with God by prayer ; as if he should say, If thou have the skill to pray continually, it will make thee rejoice continually ; for in the company of God is nothing but joy and gladness of heart.

Who ever fell into heresy, or into apostasy, or into despair, before he fell from prayer, the preservative of the soul? ' If thou hadst been here,' saith Martha to Christ, ' my brother had not died,' John xi. 32 ; so if prayer had been here, these evils had not happened. This is the holy water which driveth away unclean spirits, as Christ sheweth when he speaketh of the devil, which is ' not cast out but by fasting and prayer,' Mat. xvii. 21. This is the cross which saveth us from evil, as Christ sheweth when he teacheth us to pray (as it is written in the 11th of Luke),

'Deliver us from evil.' This is the oil which
healeth our sickness, as James sheweth in his
5th chap. ver. 25, when he saith, 'The prayer of
faith shall save the sick.' It hath such a hand in
all things, that it is like the sanctifier of everything. It blesseth our thoughts, and blesseth
our speeches, and blesseth our actions. As
Abraham blessed his servant before he went from
him, Gen. xxiv., so prayer blesseth our works
before they go from us. Whatsoever thou doest
before thou hast blessed it with prayer, thou hast no
promise that it shall prosper or do good, because
he which should bless it is not made a counsel
to it. Therefore we should not presume to use
any of God's gifts, or any of God's graces, without
prayer, lest that which is good do not good but
hurt unto us.

For this cause St Paul, in the 14th of the
Romans, and the 6th verse, teacheth us to pray
before we eat. For this cause Paul prayed
before he journeyed, Acts xx. 26, 38 ; for this
cause Elias prayed before he sacrificed, as it
appeareth in the 1st book of Kings, xviii. 36 ; for
this cause the Israelites prayed before they fought;
and for this cause we pray before we preach. It
is a good thing to preach, and yet you see we do
not presume to preach before we pray ; because
' Paul planteth, Apollos watereth ; but God giveth

the increase,' 1 Cor. iii. 6. Even so, we should not presume to give alms, nor to give counsel, nor to give help, before we have prayed that it may do good. Nay, we should not presume to exercise our faith, nor our repentance, nor our obedience, without prayer; because there is no faith so perfect but it had need of prayer to strengthen it. Also, there is no love so perfect but it had need of prayer to confirm it. There is no repentance so perfect but it had need of prayer to continue it; there is no obedience so perfect but it had need of prayer to direct it. Therefore he doth sin which presumeth to do any good work without prayer, because he seems to do it by his own power; for he that craveth not assistance from God, which giveth power to faith to bring forth works, as well as he doth to trees to bring forth fruits, or to physic to bring forth health. Therefore no virtue hath done so much as prayer hath done, for all virtues have had their power from prayer; and therefore one saith, that prayer hath done as many exploits as all virtues beside.

I have known many wicked men hear, and I have known many wicked men study, and I have known many wicked men fast, and I have known many wicked men preach, and I have known many wicked men counsel; but I did never know any wicked man that could pray well, nor any that could pray well, live wickedly. This Peter proveth in his first epistle and fourth chapter, when he saith, 'Be sober and watchful in prayer'; shewing, that all cannot pray, but they which are sober and watchful.

St Paul, in Rom. xii., teacheth us a reasonable service of God. Here he seems to enjoin us an unreasonable service of God. For who did ever pray continually? or if we should pray continually, when should we hear, or preach, or when should we study, or when should we work? So one service seems to hinder all services; but indeed it doth further all services, and therefore we are commanded to pray continually, because we can do nothing without prayer. But if you imagine that this commandment is broken if your lips be not always going, which was the heresy of the Messalians, or if you dwell not always in the church, like the golden candlesticks, then you are out of Paul's mind, for Paul did not pray continually with his lips, and therefore he doth not mean a lip prayer; neither did Paul live day and night in the temple, and therefore he doth not mean a church prayer; and further, it seems that the Jews were not appointed to pray at all times, for they had set times of prayer; and therefore we read how 'Peter and John went up to the temple at the

time of prayer,' Acts iii. 1; therefore to pray
continually, is to lift up our hearts continually
unto God, and to pray in our thought, as Moses
did, though we open not our lips; and so we
pray continually. As when a good man is to
answer before his persecutor, a thought prayeth
in his heart that he may answer wisely; when he
is to give alms, a thought prayeth in his heart
that it may do good; when he is to give counsel,
a thought prayeth in his heart that it may
prosper; when he is to hear a sermon, a thought
prayeth in his heart that he may be edified
and sanctified by it. Thus we may pray and
hear, pray and speak, pray and eat, pray and
study, pray and work together, as the Jews built
and fought together, Neh. iv. 7. And therefore
prayer seems a harder thing than it is. For if
it had been irksome for any to pray, Paul would
not have joined praying and rejoicing together.
It is not hard which a man may do and rejoice
too. If a man love entirely, he hath no such
delight as to talk often, and to confer daily with
him whom he loveth; for by this his love is
increased, and his joy is doubled; but the
seldomer we commune together, by little and
little our affections abate, till at last we become
strange one to the other, as though we had never
been acquainted. Even so our affections and

familiarity doth grow towards God by often praying unto him ; and when we leave off to pray, then our affections draw from him, and his affections from us.

Seeing, then, that prayer is such an excellent thing, that it is given to none but to him which is called *excellent* ; and such a pleasant thing, that Paul joineth *pray continually* with *rejoice continually* ; and such an heavenly thing, that it makes us like the angels which are in heaven ; and such a necessary thing, that God built a house for it, and made a day for it ; and such a holy thing, that none but the holy can deal with it ; and such a strong thing, that it overcometh God which overcometh all ; how is it, then, that our fathers spent so much time in prayer, and we make no account of it ? Have we nothing to pray for as well as they ? Nay, they prayed for nothing but we had need to pray for the like. The Turks and idolaters pray to them that cannot hear ; but he which saith, ' I will hear,' hath not so many supplications to him as noblemen. What will we give God, if we will not afford him thanks ? What will we do for him, if we will not praise him ? ' If thou be wise,' saith Solomon, ' thou art wise unto thyself'; so if we do pray, we do pray for ourselves. Shall the birds sing unto God, and not they for whom he created birds ? What a fool is he which will fight, and travel, and watch for himself, and will not speak for himself! If God had required such costly sacrifices of us as he did of the Jews, it is to be feared that he would not be served at all; for we are such Gergesites, that we would not part from our beasts to sacrifice to him. Therefore, let us not say, God will not hear, but let us say, We do not ask; for God is readier to give than we to ask. Therefore, let us pray that our neglect of prayer may be forgiven.

A LOOKING-GLASS FOR
CHRISTIANS

*I say, through the grace that is given unto me, to
every one that is among you, that no man
presume to understand above that which is
meet to understand; but that he understand
according to sobriety, as God hath dealt to
every man the measure of faith.*—Rom. xii. 3.

FIRST of the preface, and then of the counsel.
In the first verse of this chapter Paul persuadeth
the Romans 'by the mercy of God' towards *them*;
here he persuadeth them 'by the grace of God
towards *him*.' Paul speaks like a man on his
death-bed, which is set to give good counsel, and
goeth from one lesson to another, as though he
would speak all with a breath. First, he counselled them to make their bodies serve God,
because the body is a servant as well as the soul;
then he forbade them to fashion themselves to the
world, because no man can serve two contrary
masters; then he advised them to renew their
minds, because, except the mind be reformed, the

body will serve but a while ; and he setteth them to seek God's will, because the will of man doth seduce him.   And now, to make up his testament, as it were, he admonisheth them to rest in the knowledge of God's will, and not to search farther, nor to be proud of their knowledge, but to use their knowledge to humble their pride.

Five things, in my judgment, are to be noted in these words : The first is, that wisdom is a thing to be desired, for when he saith, *not above sobriety*, he would have us wise *within sobriety*. The second is, that every man affecteth a kind of wisdom, either according to sobriety, as Paul counselled the Romans, or above sobriety, as the Romans did before.   The third is, few are wise, as God counteth wisdom; and therefore Paul speaketh to all, as though all were to learn this lesson.   The fourth is, that sobriety doth shew, like a glass, who are wise, and who are not.   The last is, that the wisdom which goeth beyond sobriety doth hurt him which hath it, and others ; for when Paul saith, ' Be wise to sobriety,' he implieth, that who is not so is in a kind of distemperature, like one scarce sober.   Paul makes a general charge, ' I say to every one, Be wise according to sobriety ' ; as though every one had too much wisdom, or too little.   Virtue is a mean betwixt two vices, which couch so close beside her, that one can scarce see her; covetousness on the one side, and prodigality on the other side, and charity in the midst; pride on the one side, rusticity on the other side, and comeliness in the midst; flattery on the one side, malice on the other side, and love in the midst; carefulness on the one side, carelessness on the other side, and diligence in the midst; diffidence on the one side, presumption on the other side, and faith in the midst; superstition on the one side, atheism on the other side, and religion in the midst; ignorance on the one side, curiosity on the other side, and knowledge in the midst; so that there is but one virtue still for two vices; therefore extremities bear rule in this world. Either we cry *Hosanna*, or else *Crucifige*; either Christ must not wash our feet, or else he must wash our feet and body too; either we will have Paul a god, or else we say he is cursed of God, Acts xxviii. 4, 6; either we say, 'Touch not, taste not,' for it is unclean, or else we say, 'Let us eat and drink, for to-morrow we shall die.' If we love, we do over-love; if we fear, we over-fear; if we be careful, we be over-careful; if we be merry, we are over-merry; if we be solemn, we are over-solemn; if so, we cannot be wise, but we are over-wise; so soon as we are thought to know something, we would be thought ignorant of nothing. There is a kind of down or curdle upon wisdom, like the train of gentlewomen, which is more than needs, which we call the crotchets of the brain, which must be weeded out, as the tree is lopped when it groweth too thick ; or else they will perish in the brain, like a scum which seetheth into the broth. The Scripture speaketh of many ancient, and many rich, and many strong, and many mighty ; but of one wise man, and yet that wise man, too, before he died, stepped beyond sobriety. Therefore, even as ye look, lest other men's wisdom should deceive you, so look lest your own wisdom deceive yourselves. There is a kind of wisdom which is more contrary to wisdom than ignorance. As good corn and bad corn come both to market to be sold, and the bad would have as much money as the good ; so true wisdom and false wisdom come both, shew both, offer both, praise both.

Therefore, as God appointed the people their bounds which they might not pass, when he talked with Moses in the mount ; so he hath appointed certain precincts of wisdom, which when we transgress, we may be said to exceed our commission ; like Shimei, when he went beyond the river, which Solomon forbade him. The rail or pale of wisdom is sobriety. As wisdom is made overseer of all other virtues, so sobriety is made overseer of wisdom, to measure it forth in even portions and due seasons, that none of God's gifts be lost. As water is unto the wine, to allay the heat of it, and salt is to meat, to make it savoury ; so sobriety is to wisdom, to make it wholesome and profitable to him which hath it, and them which seek it of him. 'If thou hast found honey,' saith Solomon, 'take not too much, lest thou surfeit,' Prov. xxv. 16. Nay, if thou hast found wisdom, take not too much, lest thou surfeit. There is a surfeit of wisdom, which is the dangerousest surfeit of all other ; when a man begins, like Paul, to be puffed up, which was Aaron's and Miriam's disease, when they murmured against Moses, because they thought themselves fitter to govern than he, Num. xii. 2. No virtue is better than wisdom and humility ; but if a man be proud of his wisdom and humility, then the virtue is turned into vice. 'If the light be darkness,' saith Christ, 'how great is that darkness ! So if our humility be pride, how great is that pride ! If our knowledge be ignorance, how great is that ignorance ! Therefore, as we remember, *be wise as serpents* ; so let us remember, *be simple as doves* ; or else we drown in our wisdom, like a light that quencheth in his own tallow.

Now, that ye may know how to be wise according to sobriety, there be certain properties of this sober wisdom which I will shew you.

The first is, *not to arrogate to ourselves more than God hath given us.* As the man said, 'I believe, Lord, help my unbelief'; so the wise man may say, I understand, Lord, help my ignorance. For one thing which we know, we are ignorant of a thousand things which we should know; yet the foolish virgins would be thought as wise as their sisters.

No man can abide to be disgraced in his wit; we had rather seem wicked than simple. As every bird thinks her own birds fairest, so every man thinks his own wit ripest. 'There is a generation,' saith Solomon, 'which are pure in their own conceit, but they are not cleansed from their filthiness,' Prov. xxx. 12. So there is a generation which are wise in their own conceit, but they are not cleansed from their foolishness.

The second property is, *not to glory of anything in ourselves.*

The third property is, *not to despise others.*

The fourth property is, *to keep within our calling.* He which meddleth with that which he hath not to do with is compared to one that catcheth a dog by the ears, and dares neither hold him still nor let him go; so that he can neither go forward for want of skill, nor backward for shame. God hath given certain gifts to certain callings ; as no man can exceed his gifts, so no man should exceed his calling. It is not meet that he should be a freeman which was never a prentice, nor that he should leap into Moses's chair that never sat at Gamaliel's feet. If thou doest never so well, and be not called to it, the Scripture saith straight, 'Who hath required this of thee?' thou art an usurper of another's office. 'A fool,' saith Solomon, 'is meddling'; shewing that a wise man meddleth not but where he hath to do. We are compared to a body ; some men are like the head, and they must rule ; some are like the tongue, and they must teach ; some are like the hand, and they must work. When this order is confounded, then that cometh to pass which we read of Eve ; when the woman would lead her husband, both fell into the ditch, Gen. iii. Therefore, as Christ said, 'Who hath made me a judge over you?' Luke xii. 14, so they which are not judges should say, Who hath made me a judge? He which is not a teacher should say, Who hath made me a teacher? He which is not a ruler should say, Who hath made me a ruler? And this is a better peace-maker than the lawyer.

The fifth property is, *not to be curious in searching mysteries*. This Paul meaneth when he saith, 'Let no man presume to understand

B.   129   9

above that which is meet to understand.' The star, when it came to Christ, stood still, and went no farther ; so when we come to the knowledge of Christ, we should stand still and go no farther ; for Paul was content to 'know nothing but Christ crucified.' It is not necessary to know that which God hath not revealed ; and the well of God's secrets is so deep, that no bucket of man can sound it ; therefore we must row in shallow waters, because our boats are light, and small, and soon overturned. They which have such crotchets and circumstances in their brain, I have marked this in them, that they seldom find any room for that which they should know, but go to and fro, seeking and seeking, like them which sought Elias's body, and found it not. Let men desire knowledge of God as Solomon did ; but not desire knowledge as Eve did.

Curious questions and vain speculations are like a plume of feathers, which some will give anything for, and some will give nothing for. Paul rebuked them which troubled their heads about genealogies ; how would he reprove men and women of our days, if he did see how they busy their heads about vain questions, tracing upon the pinnacles, where they may fall, while they might walk upon the pavement without danger ? Some have a great deal more desire to learn where hell is, than to know any way how they may escape it; to hear what God did purpose before the world began, rather than to learn what he will do when the world is ended; to understand whether they shall know one another in heaven, than to know whether they belong to heaven. This rock hath made many shipwrecks, that men search mysteries before they know principles; like the Bethshemites, which were not content to see the ark, but they must pry into it, and finger it. Commonly the simplest men busy their heads about the highest matters; so that if they meet with a rough and crabbed question, like a knob in the tree, and while they hack and hew at it with their own wits to make it plain, their saw sticks fast in the cleft, and cannot get out again; at last in wrath they become like malcontents with God, as though the Scripture were not perfect, and either fall into despair, or into contempt of all. Therefore it is good to leave off learning where God hath left off teaching; for they which have an ear where God hath no tongue, hearken not unto God, but to the tempter, as Eve did to the serpent. This is the rule whereby a man may know whether his wisdom stand right.

I cannot tell how it comes to pass that no man can serve God unless he know God (for none do obey him except they which do know him), and yet it is said that there was never so much knowledge and so little goodness. Surely as Christ said to his disciples, ' O ye of little faith !' so he might say to us, O ye of little understanding ! for there is not too much wisdom, but too much ostentation ; humility is none of our virtues. They which should teach others to be wise according to sobriety, pass the bounds of sobriety themselves. Every man hath a commonwealth in his head, and travails to bring forth new fashions. As the Jews were not content with such rules as God had appointed them, but would have a king like the Gentiles ; so the wisdom of this world is to devise better orders, better laws, better titles, better callings, better discipline than God hath devised himself. 'Every plant,' saith Christ, ' which my Father hath not planted shall be rooted up'; that is, every title, and every office, and every calling which God hath not planted, shall be rooted up. To be wise according to this book, is to be wise according to sobriety. Therefore seek the wisdom of Christ, for the wisdom of the serpent is turned into a curse, the wisdom of the pharisees is turned into a woe, the wisdom of Ahithophel is turned to folly, the wisdom of Nimrod is turned to confusion, the wisdom of the steward is turned to expulsion, the wisdom of Jezebel is turned to death. This is the end of the deceiver's wisdom, of the extortioner's wisdom, of the usurer's wisdom, of the persecutor's wisdom, of the flatterer's wisdom, of the sorcerer's wisdom, of the hypocrite's wisdom, of the Machiavellian's wisdom. As Moses's serpent devoured the sorcerer's serpent, so God's wisdom shall devour man's wisdom.

Wherefore, 'By the grace of God which is given unto me, I say unto every one of you,' with Paul, 'Be wise unto sobriety.' Be not ashamed to seem ignorant of some things, but remember that it is better to seem ignorant, than to be proud. Thus you have heard what wisdom is ; now let us pray unto God for it.

A CAVEAT FOR CHRISTIANS

*Let him that thinketh he stands take heed lest he
fall.*—1 Cor. x. 12.

THUS the apostle warneth us, that we are all
in a house ready to fall, all in a ship ready to sink,
and all in a body ready to sin. Who can say
what he will do when he is tried? Therefore
Paul saith not, Let him that standeth take heed
lest he fall, but 'Let him that *thinketh* he standeth
take heed lest he fall': warning us before that we
take heed of falling, and to examine how we
stand, whether we stand or no. For when he
makes his speech of them which 'think they stand,'
not of them which stand, he intends that few
stand in comparison of them which think they
stand. Many think themselves wise, that are
fools like others ; as many think themselves pure,
which are profane like others. Solomon noteth,
Prov. xxx. 12, 'There is a generation which are
pure in their own conceit, and yet are not washed
from their filthiness'; as though there were a

generation or sect of such men. And again,
Prov. xx. 6, 'Many men will boast of their
goodness, but who can find a faithful man?' So,
many seem to stand, which stand not ; many
think they believe, which know not what faith
meaneth ; many look to be saved, which cannot
tell who shall save them, no more than Nicodemus
knew what it was to be born again. The reason
is, many are afraid to sound too deep, and examine
their conscience, lest it should upbraid them with
the noisomeness of their sins. Therefore, as a
favourable judge, which would save the malefactor,
will ask him so cunningly, that he will answer for
him too ; and then he will say, I find no fault in
this man, let him pay his fees and be gone ; so
will such a man say, I find no fault in this faith ;
methinks it is a sound faith, methinks it is a good
faith, methinks it is religion enough, when I come
to the church, and love my neighbour, and obey
my prince, and give every man his own, and pay my
tithes, and fast twice a-week, as the pharisee did ;
methinks this is well, what would you have more?
Have I not kept all the commandments? Luke
xviii. 21. 'No,' saith Christ, 'there is one thing
behind'; examine thyself, and still thou shalt find
something behind, like a cobweb in the top of an
house when the floor is swept. Therefore well
does Paul say, 'he that thinketh that he stands,'

135

not he which stands; for he which stands in
Christ falleth not; but he which thinketh he
stands falleth suddenly, and may finally, unless
he stand upon his watch. *Take heed* is a good
staff to stay upon, and so often a man sins as he
casts it from him; all go astray.

But this is the difference between the sins of
them which have faith, and them which have no
faith. They which have no faith fall like an
elephant, which, when he is down, riseth not
again; they which have faith do but trip and
stumble, fall and rise again. Their falls do teach
them to stand, their weakness doth teach them
strength, their sins do teach them repentance, their
frailness teacheth them constancy, as Peter was
better after his denial than he was before. Judas
did never stand, but seemed to stand; the
disciples knew not that he was a thief, for they
asked, 'Is it I? Is it I?' Christ knew, as it
appeareth, when he gave him the sop, and said,
'That which thou doest, do quickly.' If ever
he had stood, he could not have been termed
'the son of perdition.' Many did seem to the
world to go out of the church, but John saith they
were never of the church; meaning, that if they
had been of the church, they could not have gone
out of it; for the true vine could not leave her
grapes, nor the olive her fatness, nor the fig-tree

136

her sweetness ;—so they which stand in the faith do not fall away, but seem to fall, as hypocrites seem to stand. The best men have had their slips, but always they rose again, as though they had sinned to teach us repentance ; therefore their sins are written, which else should have been concealed for their honour.

'How are the mighty overthrown,' saith David. Like Peter, which said he would never forsake Christ, and forsook him first. The strong men are fallen, even Solomon himself, and David, and Noah, and Lot, and Samson, and Peter, the lights of the world, fell like stars of heaven. These tall cedars, strong oaks, fair pillars, lie in the dust, whose tops glittered in the air, that they which think they stand, may take heed lest they fall. Who am I that I should stand like a shrub when these cedars are blown down to the ground, and shewed themselves but men? Let no man say what he will be, before he have examined what he is, but run his course with a trembling fear, always looking down to the rubs which lie before him and the worthies that are slain already.

This is the profit we should make of other men's faults, like a pearl which is taken out of the serpent ; when we see our brother's nakedness, it should move us to compassion of him, and a fear of ourselves. For when we rejoice at another's

fall, like Ham, as the leprosy went from Naaman
to Gehazi, so God 'turneth his wrath from them,'
and it lighteth upon us, Prov. xxiv. 17, 18, and
such as have despised others without remorse,
have fallen in the like, or more shamefully,
themselves, and never rose again. What shall
we do then when we hear of other men's faults?
Not talk as we do, but beware by them, and think,
Am I better than he? am I stronger than Samson?
am I wiser than Solomon? am I chaster than
David? am I soberer than Noah? am I firmer
than Peter, if God should leave me to myself, if
he should withdraw his hand which holds me?
Into how many gulfs have I been falling, when
God hath prevented me of occasion, or delayed
the temptation, or wonderfully kept me from it, I
know not how? for he delivereth me from evil, as
he delivered David from the blood of Nabal by
Abigail, which came unlooked for. So he hath
prevented many wonderfully, when they were
assaulted so hardly, that they thought to have
yielded to the enemy. Sometime I may say there
wanted a tempter, sometime I may say there
wanted time, sometime I may say there wanted
place; sometime the tempter was present, and
there wanted neither time nor place, but God held
me back that I should not consent: so near we
have glided by sin, like a ship which rides upon a

138

rock, and slips away, or a bird which scapes from the fowler when the net is upon her. There is no salt but may lose his saltness, no wine but may lose his strength, no flower but may lose his scent, no light but may be eclipsed, no beauty but may be stained, no fruit but may be blasted, nor soul but may be corrupted. We stand all in a slippery place, where it is easy to slide, and hard to get up ; like little children, which overthrow themselves with their clothes, now up, now down at a straw, so soon we fall from God, and slide from his word, and forget our resolutions, as though we had never resolved. Man goeth forth in the morning, weak, naked, and unarmed, to fight with powers and principalities, the devil, the world, and all their adherents ; and whom doth he take with him but his flesh, a traitor, ready to yield up at every assault unto the enemy? Thus man is set upon the side of a hill, always declining and slipping ; the flesh muffleth him to make him stumble, the world catcheth at him to make him fall, the devil undermineth him to make him sink, and crieth still, Cast thyself down ; and when he falleth, he goeth apace, as Peter, who denieth thrice together ; and when he is fallen, is like a stumbling-stone in the way for others, that they may fall too. Therefore, ' Let him that thinketh he standeth, take heed lest he fall.'

139

So earnestly must we call upon our souls, that we be not weary of well-doing ; for happier are the children that never began, than Judas, whose end was worse than his beginning. Wisdom and righteousness are angry with him that leaveth his goodness to become worse. If thou wert like the vine, or the olive, or the fig-tree, they would not leave their grapes, or their fatness, or their sweetness, to get a kingdom, but the bramble did. If thou be like the bramble, what wilt thou do when the fire comes? As this is a memorandum to all, so especially let him that ruleth, and him that teacheth, take heed lest he fall ; for if the pillars shrink, the temple shakes. As when a great tree is hewn down, which is a shadow to the beasts, and a nest to the birds, many leaves, and boughs, and twigs fall with it ; so many stand and fall with them whose lamps give light to others, even as Jeroboam's sin made Israel to sin. Therefore Paul hath given you a watchword, which every one should write upon his table, upon his bed, and upon his nails, lest he forget in one hour ; for he which stands now may fall before night. Sin is not long in coming, nor quickly gone, unless God stop us, as he met Balaam in his way, and stay us, as he stayed the woman's son, when he was a-bearing to his grave. We run over reason, and tread upon conscience, and fling by counsel, and go by the word, and post to death, as though we ran for a kingdom. Like a lark, that falls to the ground sooner than she mounted up; at first she retires as it were by steps, but when she cometh nearer the ground, she falls down with a jump; so we decline at first, and waver lower and lower, till we be almost at the worst, and then we run headlong, as though we were sent post to hell : from hot to lukewarm, from lukewarm to key-cold, from key-cold to stark dead ; so the languishing soul bleeds to death, and seeth not his life go, till he be at the very last gasp. Woe be unto him that is guilty of this murder ! If the blood of Abel cried for vengeance against his brother Cain, which slew his body, shall not God be revenged for the death of his soul? 'Where is thy brother?' saith God. Nay, where is thy soul? hast thou slain it, which was my spouse, my temple, mine own image?

141

JACOB'S LADDER; OR, THE WAY
TO HEAVEN

So run, that ye may obtain.—1 Cor. ix. 24.

BECAUSE I have but one hour to teach you all
that you must learn of me, I have chosen a text
which is like Jacob's ladder, that shews you the
way to heaven. This is all that you would know;
and it may please God to open your eyes, that
you may know it before ye depart. Hear to
practise; hinder not the Spirit, but let it work
without resistance; record when you are gone,
and you shall see the great power of God, what he
is able to do for you by one sentence of this book,
if ye digest it well. 'So run, that ye may obtain.'
If many run and do not obtain, how easy is it to
run in vain! and how happy is he which obtaineth
that that all men wish, when so many miss it for
nothing but for this, because they run out of the
way! You have heard, read, and done much, and
more would do, to obtain eternal life with the
angels in heaven; for this you pray, and fast, and
watch, and obey the laws of God, and come

together every Sabbath to hear, to pray, to praise, and serve him which giveth it. How many prayers, how many fasts, how many watches, how many works, how many hours in reading the word, in hearing the word, in receiving the sacrament, in examining your heart, in chastising your flesh, were spent and lost, if you should run in vain! as Esau hunted for a blessing, and went without it. Therefore the Holy Ghost doth say nothing, but it is like a mark in our way, to shew us when we are in, and when we are out; for God would not have us lose our labour, like Laban, which could find in his heart, after Jacob had served him twenty years, to send him away empty; but he would have you to 'seek and find,' to 'ask and receive,' to 'run and obtain'; therefore he saith, 'So run, that ye may obtain.' As there is a heaven, so there is a way to heaven; one way Adam came from paradise, and by another he must return to paradise. The passage is not so stopped but there is a way, though a strait way, and a door, though it be a narrow door, and therefore few do find it; only they which are like Jacob do see a ladder before them, as Jacob did. He had many dreams before, and did not see it; at last 'he dreamed, and, behold, a ladder which reached from earth to heaven, and all the angels descended and ascended by it,' to shew that no man ascendeth to heaven but by that ladder. This ladder is Christ, which saith, 'I am the way,' and therefore he bids us to follow him. If we must follow Christ his steps, let us see how he went to heaven. He begun betime, for at twelve years of age he said, 'I must go about my Father's business,' Luke ii. 49. He made speed; for John saith that 'He spake and did more good things,' in three and thirty years, 'than could be written,' John xxi. 25. He kept the right way; for when he said, 'Who can accuse me of sin?' none could accuse him of any, though they watched him for that purpose. He continued well; for he died like a lamb, and prayed to his Father, and forgave his enemies. Therefore we will call the steps of this ladder, *Maturè, properè, rectè, constanter*; that is, *Begin betime, Make haste, Keep the way,* and *Hold to the end,* and thou shalt go after thy Master.

Touching the first, *Begin betime.* God requiring the first-born for his offering. The best season to seek God is to seek him early. And therefore Wisdom saith, 'They that seek me early shall find me'; but to them which defer, she saith, 'Ye shall seek me but shall not find me.' Who is so young that has not received some talent or other? Therefore youth cannot excuse him, because the talent requires to be used of every one

that hath it. This made David to cry, 'Remember
not the sins of my youth,' Ps. xxv. 7, which he
would not have spoken, if God did not mark the
sins of youth as well as age. Therefore the fathers
were charged to teach their children the same law
which they had themselves, Deut. vi. 7. Therefore
Christ rebuked the disciples which forbade the
little children to be brought to him, Mat. xix. 14;
for, should children honour their father, and not
honour God? It was a sweet concert when the
children went before Christ to the temple and
sung their *Hosanna*, to make their fathers ashamed,
which did not know the Messias when he came,
when their little children knew him. It is written,
when Christ heard a young man answer that he
had kept the commandments from his youth,
Christ began to love him, Mark x. 20, 21; which
shews how Christ loves these timely beginnings,
when we make him our nurse, and draw our first
milk from his breasts. There is not one confession
for old men, and another for young men; in the
Creed, the old man saith not, I *did* believe in God,
and the young man saith not, I *will* believe in
God; but both say, I *do* believe in God. For he
which is called I AM, Exod. iii. 14, loveth *I am*,
and careth not for *I was*, nor *I will be*. When
Christ asked Peter, 'Lovest thou me?' John xxi.
15, he looked that he should answer him, 'Yea,

Lord, I love thee'; and not drive off as Felix did Paul, Acts xxiv. 25, 'I will hear thee,' I will love thee, 'when I have time convenient': nay, when thou hast not convenient time, for if this be the convenient time, after this the convenient time is past. Manna was gathered in the morning, because when the sun arose it did melt away ; so virtue must be gathered betime, for if we stay till business and pleasures come upon us, they will melt it faster than we can gather it. If thou lackest a spur to make thee run, see how every day runneth away with thy life ; youth cometh upon childhood, age cometh upon youth, death cometh upon age, with such a swift sail, that if our minutes were spent in mortifying ourselves, yet our glass would be run out before we had purged half our corruptions. Thus much of the first step.

The second step in your journey is, to *keep the way*. As God taught the Israelites the way to Canaan, sending a fiery pillar before them, which they did follow wheresoever it went ; so when he ordained a heaven for men, he appointed a way to come unto it, which way he that misseth shall never come to the end. As Herod sought Christ over all Jewry, but none found him but those which followed the star, Mat. ii. ; so there is something still that leadeth men to Christ, which we must follow, or else we cannot come where he is. There be many wrong ways, as there be many errors ; there is but one right way, as there is but one truth. And, therefore, Jacob did not see many, but one ladder, which reached to heaven ; and John Baptist is said, not to 'prepare the *ways* of the Lord,' but 'the *way*,' shewing that there is but one right way in this life ; which Solomon understandeth for the mean, and therefore he said, 'Turn not to the right hand nor to the left,' implying that we may err as well of the right hand as of the left. As if he should say, Some are too hot, as others are too cold ; some are too superstitious, as others are too careless ; some are too fearful, as others are too confident ; there is a zeal without knowledge, a love without singleness, a prayer without faith, and a faith without fruits. Therefore the apostle doth warn us to 'examine whether we be in the faith,' 2 Cor. xiii. 5 ; not whether we have a kind of faith, but whether we be *in the faith*, *i.e.* the true faith. Therefore Paul saith, *Run so*. It is not enough to run, but we must know how we run ; it is not enough to hear, but we must care how we hear ; it is not enough to believe, but we must care how we believe ; it is not enough to pray, but we must care how we pray ; it is not enough to work, but we must care how we work, for we cannot do good unless we do it well.

Now when you are in the way, it's good to make speed ; therefore the next step in your journey is, *Make haste.* For this cause Paul saith, *Run*, which is the swiftest pace of man ; as though he should go faster to heaven than to any place else in the world. His meaning is this, that as a man doth watch, and run, and labour, to be rich quickly, so he should hear, and pray, and study, and use all means, to be wise quickly. This the apostle understandeth when he biddeth us to *add* ; as if he should say, When thou art in the way, and knowest good from evil, every day kill some vice, and every week sow some virtue, and make thy two talents five talents, thy five talents ten talents, and ever be doing ; and at last it shall be opened to thee, because thou hast knocked. Christ saith, 'The kingdom of heaven is got by violence,' Mat. xi. 12 ; therefore a man must be earnest and zealous in the religion that he professes, or else it makes no matter of what religion he is, for, if he be but lukewarm, God threateneth to spue him out of his mouth, Rev. iii. 15, 16. Every man hath a kind of religion, and the religion of most is to be like one another,— as merciful as others, as humble as others, as devout as others ; but God saith, ' Be holy, as I am,' not as others are ; for Christ saith, ' Except your righteousness exceed the righteousness of

148

the pharisees,' although they were holier than others, 'ye shall not enter into heaven'; that is, except ye be more than statute-protestants, which go to the church, and hear an homily, and receive once a year, but will not offend any person, nor leave any custom, nor bear any charge, nor suffer any trouble for the glory of God, ye shall come to heaven when the pharisees come out of hell. As love delighteth men, so zeal pleaseth God, for zeal is the love of God. Therefore every sacrifice was offered with fire, to shew with what zeal they should burn which come to offer prayer or praise or thanks unto the Lord; therefore the Holy Ghost descends in fire, to shew the fervency of them upon whom the Holy Ghost resteth; therefore the cherubims were pourtrayed with wings before the people, to shew that they should be as earnest and quick about the Lord's business as the cherubims; therefore God would not take a lame nor halting sacrifice, to shew how he abhorreth slackness in all our duties; therefore St James says, 'Be swift to hear,' James i. 19. We must be swift to pray, swift to obey, swift to do good; for he is not cursed only which doeth not the Lord's business, but he which 'doeth it negligently,' Jer. xlviii. 10, *i.e.* he which doeth anything before it, like him that would bid his friends farewell, and follow Christ after, Luke ix. 61.

The hound, which runs but for the hare, runs as fast as possibly he can ; the hawk, which flieth but for the partridge, flieth as fast as possibly she can ; and shall he which runs for heaven creep more slowly than the dial ?

The fourth step in this happy journey is, *Persevere to the end.* There is nothing in our life which suffers so many eclipses and changes as our devotion ; hot and cold, in and out, off and on, not in one mood so long as the sparrow sits on the ground, but looking like the chameleon, of the colour of that which we see : if we see good, it puts us in a good thought ; if we see or hear evil, it turns us from good to evil again. Thus man is rolled upon a wheel that never stands still, but turns continually about, as though he were giddy and treading the maze. He is upon the side of a hill where it is easy to slide, and hard to get up the flesh. Therefore the apostle, moved with pity, seeing man stand on such a slippery ground, as it were in a ship ready to sink, or a house bending to fall, he cries to them that stand surest, 'Take heed lest you fall' ; *i.e.* when thou hast put on thy 'armour of light,' and art in the spiritual field to fight the Lord's battles against the world, the flesh, and the devil, turn not back like Demas, but remember the comfort of Elisha, that 'there be more with thee than against thee,'

and that the tempter can overcome none but
them which yield. Other servants change their
masters for better masters ; but all that serve God
are like the servant which received a print in
his ear after the manner of the Jews, in token
that he would serve his master for ever, like the
vestures which bare their own mark. Therefore
the Holy Ghost cries so often, ' Be faithful even
unto the death,' ' Be not weary of well-doing,'
' Take heed lest you fall.' For when thou art
weary of thy godliness, God doth not count thee
good, but weary of goodness ; and when thou
declinest from righteousness, God doth not count
thee righteous, but revolted from righteousness.
Therefore Paul saith, 'Pray continually,' as though
prayer were nothing without continuance. Jacob
did not overcome God so soon as he began to
wrestle with him, but when he had wrestled with
him all night. And it is said that Christ took
pity of them that stayed with him. ' I will not
leave thee,' saith Elisha to Elijah ; so we should
not leave God. Some came into the vineyard
in the morning, and some at noon ; but none
received any reward but they which stayed till
night. As God's mercy endureth for ever, so our
righteousness should endure for ever. Every
thought, and word, and deed of a faithful man is
a step towards heaven ; in every place he meeteth

Christ, everything puts him in mind of God; he seeks him to find him, and when he hath found him, he seeks him still; he is not satisfied, because at every touch there comes some virtue from him. If men did bend themselves as much to do good as they beat their brains to do evil, they might go to heaven with less trouble than they go to hell. Our idle hours are enough to get wisdom, and knowledge, and faith, till we are like saints among men. If thou look only to the stops, and tell all the thorns which lie in the way, thou shalt go fearfully, wearily, and unwillingly, everything shall turn thee aside, and every snail shall step before thee, and take thy crown from thee; but then lift up thine eyes from the earth, and look to Christ calling, the Spirit assisting, the Father blessing, the angels comforting, the word directing, the crown inviting, and thy fetters shall fall from thee, and thou shalt rise like the sun, and marvel how the thing could seem so hard, and be so easy. When ye do well, remember that ye change not for the worse, and do as ye do then, and ye shall continue to the end.

Now I have encouraged you like soldiers, and taken away your fear, I will bring you to the sight of your enemies, and will set them before your face; not to weaken you, for that were want of charity, but to make you wary, which is true love indeed. To number them surely I cannot, they are so many, and exactly to describe them, it is beyond my skill, they are so subtle ; howbeit, to give you a little taste, I may say as Elisha said to his servant, and you shall see it, if you have your eyes open, 'Fear not, for they that be with us are more than they that be with them' ; and he that is on our side is stronger than all. But if you will hear what the holy apostle saith touching them, I can tell you ; he affirmeth, and that by the very Spirit of God, 'We wrestle not against flesh and blood only, but against principalities, powers, worldly governors, the princes of the darkness of this world, even spiritual wickedness in the high places,' Eph. vi. 12. And St John saith, 'They are the lusts of the flesh, the lusts of the eyes, and the pride of life,' 1 John ii. 16. Let other men think of them what they list ; they that hear them thus described, and have felt the force of them in their own souls, could not choose but confess that they have been many in number, mighty in power, subtle in practice, and what not. Who knoweth not this, that the more enemies we have the more need we have both of force outwardly, and of care inwardly? as again, the more powerful they are, and the more weak we are, the more we should seek for help elsewhere.

But whom shall we look to herein? Other men are as weak as ourselves, if not worse; for all men, 'lay them upon a balance, they are altogether lighter than vanity itself,' Ps. lxii. 9. And if we fear and distrust ourselves, how dare we, or how can we, put confidence in others? specially sith God saith, 'Cursed is every one that maketh flesh and blood his arm,' Jer. xvii. 5. To look up to the holy and elect angels will do us little good; because they go not but being sent, and always wait for a word and warrant from the Lord's own mouth for all their actions; besides that, their own oil and force is little enough for their own supportation. To God, therefore, that is the God of our strength, we must needs come; yea, and to him alone, or else we are utterly overthrown and cast away. And if we cannot say, and do too, as David did, 'Lord, whom have I in heaven but thee? and I have desired none on earth with thee,' we are in a woful taking, and utterly lost. For fear without and fire within, Satan's malice also, men's mischief, and our corruption, will carry and hurry us, as it were a violent tempest or whirlwind. To bring all into a sum, I say, let all objected be as true as anything may be, yet all these, and a thousand more such like, are nothing to him that is in Christ. For the apostle saith, 'There is no condemnation

154

to them that are in Christ Jesus,' Rom. viii. 1 ;
and it is he alone that hath destroyed death, and
'became sin for us, that we in him might be made
the righteousness of God.' And surely such a one
may in some good measure of comfort joyfully say,
to the defiance even of death itself, and all other
ghostly enemies whatsoever, 'O death, where is
thy sting? O grave, where is thy victory? The sting
of death is sin, and the strength of sin is the law.'
Wherefore let us not fear all or any of our adversaries or pull-backs, for 'true love expelleth fear,'
1 John iv. 18 ; neither let us be faint-hearted in
ourselves, but labour rather to 'lift up our hands
which hang down, and to strengthen our weak
knees,' Heb. xii. 12 ; for 'faithful is he that hath
promised, who will also perform it,' Heb. x. 23.
'Be faithful unto death, and I will give thee the
crown of life,' Rev. ii. 10. He that so runneth,
shall be sure to obtain, and have his portion with
the saints in the heavenly inheritance, of a crown
that never fadeth nor falleth away. Wherefore,
as you love life, and loathe death, run well, I
beseech you ; yea, even as our text was at the
beginning, so say I at the ending, 'So run, that
ye may obtain.' Which I do not only propound
unto you by exhortation, but commend and
commit, with supplication to God for myself and
you, that every one of us, and I myself especially,

155

may in feeling and faith say, ' I am now ready to be offered, and the time of my departing is at hand ; I have fought a good fight, and have finished my course, I have kept the faith. From hence is laid up for me the crown of righteousness, which the Lord, the righteous judge, shall give me at that day ; and not to me only, but unto all them that love his appearing,' 2 Tim. iv. 6–8.

THE LAWYER'S QUESTION
AND THE LAWGIVER'S ANSWER

And behold, a certain lawyer stood up and
tempted him, saying, Master, what shall I
do to inherit eternal life ? And he said unto
him, What is written in the law ? how readest
thou ? &c.—Luke x. 25, 26.

IT is a weighty question, and hath been long
discoursed, by what means a man may come to
heaven ; and who is not desirous to be resolved in
it ? Here the question is propounded by a lawyer,
and answered by the Lawgiver, whose judgment
in this case is worth the hearing. He propounds
the question as one desirous to learn, when indeed
he meaneth nothing less. But as Ahab, when he
asked Micaiah, in the first book of Kings and 22nd
chapter, if he should go up to fight against
Ramoth in Gilead, meant not to follow the
prophet's direction, but only desired to hear his
opinion ; so the lawyer propounds this question,

not with a mind to learn of Christ, but with a mind to tempt Christ, and to try his learning.

Of all kind of cattle these are the worst, because they do most hurt where they are least mistrusted. Therefore they are compared in Scripture to the wily fox, for their crafty fetches. And Herod is termed a fox for his dissembling, Luke xiii. 32. For as the fox feigneth himself dead, that he may catch the birds to devour them, so the flatterer feigneth himself to be harmless, and honest, and conscionable, and religious, and holy, that he may 'deceive the hearts of the simple,' Rom. xvi. 18. He is like your shadow, which doth imitate the action and gesture of your body, which stands when you stand, and walks when you walk, and sits when you sit, and riseth when you rise; so the flatterer doth praise when you praise, and finds fault when you find fault, and smiles when you smile, and frowns when you frown, and applauds you in your doings, and soothes you in your sayings, and in all things seeks to please your humour, till he hath sounded the depth of your devices, that he may betray you to your greatest enemies. As the sirens sing most sweetly when they intend your destruction, so flatterers speak most fair when they practise most treachery. Therefore every fair look is not to be liked, every smooth tale is not to be believed, and

158

every glozing tongue is not to be trusted ; but as we must 'try the spirits, whether they be of God or no,' I John iv. I, so we must try the words, whether they come from the heart or no ; and we must try the deeds, whether they be answerable to the words or no.

Now we are come to the question, which is, 'By what means may a man inherit eternal life?' A weighty question, worthy to be known, not only of lawyers and learned men, but also of all, both men and women, which be persuaded in their hearts, as with their mouth they do confess, that after death their bodies shall rise again. Therefore, though this lawyer were to be blamed, because he came with so bad a mind, yet is he to be commended, because he moved so good a question. Many now-a-days are very curious in idle and unprofitable questions, as, What God did before he made the world? How long Adam stood in the state of innocency? Whether Solomon were saved or no? with many such vain and unnecessary questions. But few there are which will ask, as this lawyer did, what they must do to inherit eternal life. You shall see many very careful and inquisitive how they may get riches, where they may purchase lands and lordships, how they may come to advancement and honour, and by what means they may procure the prince's favour. But we shall see few or none inquisitive concerning the means of their salvation ; you shall seldom hear any ask their pastor what they must do to be saved, or which way they may come. This man was a pharisee, such a one as Paul was before his conversion, one that expounded the law of God to the people and lived after the straitest law of their religion ; in a word such a one as both for his life and learning was admired and honoured of the Jews. Though this lawyer was learned, yet it was boldly done of him to tempt the Lord. But what is it that learning dare not attempt, if it be not tempered with the fear of God ? Christ Jesus found no greater adversaries than the high priests and scribes and pharisees, which were all learned men ; and the church of Christ at this day is by none so much afflicted as by those that carry of singular learning. For look how many heresies are extant in the church, or how many controversies in religion that have been devised and are maintained by learned men. Let learned men therefore learn to fear the Lord ; let them learn to 'know nothing so much as Christ Jesus and him crucified,' 1 Cor. ii. 2, without which knowledge all knowledge is ignorance, all wisdom is foolishness, all learning is madness, and all religion is error, or hypocrisy, or superstition. Our Saviour Christ, in the choice

of his apostles, called not one that was learned ;
yet hath he not rejected all that are learned, for
from heaven he called his apostle Paul, a learned
lawyer, Acts xxii. 3, to be the apostle and the
preacher of the Gentiles, Rom. xi. 13. And there
is no doubt but that in all ages, and even at this
day, he calleth some in every place, and endueth
them with excellent learning, that they may serve
to 'the gathering together of the saints, and to
the exercising of the ministry, and to the edifying
of the church of God,' Eph. iv. 12.

*Good Master, what shall I do to inherit eternal
life?* Mark here the discretion of the lawyer in
asking this question. As the man was a lawyer,
so there is no doubt but that he had read the law
and the prophets. If you look into the law, you
shall not find, 'Cursed is he that continueth not
in all things that are written in the book of the
law, to know them.' If you peruse the prophets,
you shall not find, 'Cease from doing evil, and
learn to speak well.' But the law saith, 'Cursed
is he which continueth not in all things that are
written in the book of the law, to do them,'
Deut. xxvii.

What shall I do to inherit eternal life? There
is a life which is short and temporal, which Job
compareth to a wind, that soon bloweth over, Job
vii. 7 ; James to a vapour, that soon vanisheth

away, James iv. 14. This lawyer asks not after his temporal life, for this is common to beasts with men; but here he inquireth concerning that life which is eternal, and shall never have an end. It is strange to see how every man almost desireth to be eternal, and yet how few do use the means to be eternal. As the fowls by a natural inclination delight to fly, the fish to swim, and the beasts to go, so men are naturally carried with an earnest desire to live for ever.

To the obtaining of eternal life two things are necessary. The first is, to believe well; the second is, to live well. By the first we are justified in the sight of God, for he respects our faith; by the second we are justified in the sight of men, for they regard our works. And thus are the apostles Paul and James reconciled. For when Paul maketh faith the cause of justification, Rom. iii. 28, he meaneth such a faith as 'worketh by love,' Gal. v. 6, whereby we are justified in the sight of God. And when James maketh works the cause of justification, James ii. 24, he meaneth such works as proceed from faith, James ii. 18, whereby we are declared to be righteous before men.

The Scripture describeth this eternal life by divers excellent names, to shew the worthiness and excellency thereof. It is called 'a kingdom,'

Luke xii. 32, but yet such a kingdom as 'cannot be shaken,' not like the kingdoms of this world, Heb. xii. 28, for it is 'an heavenly kingdom,' Mat. viii. 11. It is called 'paradise,' Luke xxiii. 43, for it is more pleasant than the garden of Eden. And 'Abraham's bosom,' Luke xvi. 22, for it is a place of rest and comfort. It is called 'the house of the Father, wherein there be many mansions,' John xiv. 2; 'the joy of the Lord,' whereinto every faithful servant must enter, Mat. xxv. 21; and all to express and declare unto us the beauty, excellency, and glory of that life which is eternal. And yet as glorious and excellent as it is, such is the love and favour of God unto us, that he hath appointed it to be our inheritance, as here the lawyer termeth it. Inheritance is a kind of tenure, whereby a man in his own right holdeth or possesseth any thing as his own; as when a lawful heir doth inherit his father's lands; even so the kingdom of God belongeth unto us, as our lawful inheritance, because we are the sons of God.

It is a great prerogative to be 'the son of God,' John i. 12. But to be heirs, and heirs with Christ, Rom. viii. 17, of that heavenly inheritance, is a wonderful privilege. How are we bound unto almighty God, that whereas he might have made us stones, or trees, or beasts, or such insensible and unreasonable creatures, it pleased his divine majesty to make us men, the undoubted heirs of eternal happiness! Behold, dear brother, and consider that heaven is thine inheritance, eternal glory is thy patrimony; thou art born to a kingdom, thou hast a title to it, and when thou dost depart this life thou shalt be sure to find it, if before thou depart this life thou do not lose thy right and title by thy sinful life.

Now you have heard the question propounded, you shall hear the question answered: 'And he said unto him, What is written in the law? how readest thou?' as if he should have said, I marvel that thou, being a doctor of the law, which should be able to instruct others in matters of religion, art ignorant of that which it behoveth every man to know, by what means he may inherit eternal life. Wherein hast thou bestowed thy study? wherein hast thou employed thy wit? and how hast thou spent thy time? Thou seemest to be a lawyer: tell me, what doth the law require of thee? Thou seemest to have read the Scriptures: let me see how thou hast profited by thy reading. Thus doth our Saviour send this lawyer to the law to learn his duty, and setteth him to school, that thought himself too good to learn. He came to tempt Christ by asking the question; but now himself must make the answer, unless he will bewray his own ignorance.

It followeth, ver. 27, 'And he answered and said, Thou shalt love thy Lord God with all thy heart, and with all thy soul, and with all thy strength, and with all thy thought; and thy neighbour as thyself.' The lawyer in his answer sheweth himself a learned lawyer; for whereas the law of God consisteth of ten precepts, he reduceth the same unto two.

Here is nothing but love (my brethren) and yet here is the fulfilling of the law. For all the benefits that God had bestowed upon the Israelites, his people, he requireth nothing but love; and for all favours which he hath done unto us, he asketh no more but love again. He asketh love; a kind of service which every man may well afford. He asketh not learning, nor strength, nor riches, nor nobility, but he asketh love; a thing that the simplest, the weakest, the poorest, the basest may perform, as well as he that is most learned, most strong, most rich, or most nobly born. If God had required this of thee, that thou shouldst be able to dissolve doubts, like Daniel, and to dispute subtle questions, what should then become of thee that art unlearned? If the Lord should accept of none but such as were strong and valiant, what should then become of women, old men, and children, which are weak and feeble? If God should regard none but the rich and wealthy, what should then become of the poor and needy? To conclude, if God should make choice of none but such as were of noble parentage, what should we do that are the common people? But now he requireth such a thing of us, as the poorest and simplest may perform as well as the wealthiest or wisest man in all the world ; for if we cannot love, we can do nothing; especially if we cannot love God, that hath so loved us, we go not so far as the wicked do, for 'sinners also love their lovers,' Luke vi. 32. And therefore blessed be God, that for the performance of so small a work, hath proposed such a great reward ; and for the obtaining of such a happy state, hath imposed such an easy task. 'The eye hath not seen, the ear hath not heard, neither can the heart conceive, what God hath prepared for them that love him,' Isa. lxiv. 4, and 1 Cor. ii. 9. And for all these unspeakable joys which God hath prepared, he requires no more of us but love. How is God enamoured of our love? and how unkind shall we be to withhold it from him? He hath an innumerable company of angels, which are inflamed with his love ; and not content therewith, he sues to have the love of men. God hath no need of our love, no more than Elisha had need of Naaman's cleansing ; but as Elisha bade Naaman wash, that he might become clean, 2 Kings v. 10, so God bids us love, that we might be saved. It is for our good altogether that God requires our love in earth, because he means to set his love on us in heaven. If the man of God had willed Naaman to do some great thing, ought he not to have done it? So if God had willed us to do some great thing, ought we not to have done it? How much more when he saith unto us, Love, and you shall live for ever?

Now, if you would know whether you have this love of God in you, examine your actions, whether they be done with delight and comfort. *In amore nihil amari*, in love there is no mislike. It is like the waters of Jordan wherein Naaman washed; for as his flesh, which before was leprous, became fair and tender after his washing, so all our actions, and labours, and afflictions, which before were tedious and irksome, become joyous, and pleasant, and comfortable, after we are once bathed in the love of God. It is like the salt that Elisha cast into the noisome waters, to make them wholesome, 2 Kings ii. 21, or like the meal that Elisha put into the bitter pottage to make it sweet, as in 2 Kings iv. 41. So the love of God being shed in our hearts by the Holy Ghost, doth make all anguish, and sickness, and poverty, and labours, and watchings, and losses, and injuries, and famishment, and banishment, and persecutions, and imprisonment, yea, and death itself, to be welcome unto us. Such was the love of that chosen vessel, who, for the love that he bare unto God, waded through all these afflictions, 2 Cor. xi. 23, &c., and xii. 10, and could not for all these, and many more, be separated from the love of God, as he protesteth, Rom. viii. 38, 39.

Wherefore, beloved, seeing God, that hath done so much for us, requires no more but love of us, which every one may easily afford, let him be our love, our joy, and whole delight, and then our life will seem delightful. As Jacob served seven years for Rachel, Gen. xxix. 20, and 'they seemed to him but a few days, for the love that he bare unto her'; so when we have once set our love upon God, our pain will be pleasure, our sorrow will be joy, our mourning will be mirth, our service will be freedom, and all our crosses will be counted so many comforts, for his sake whom we love a great deal more than Jacob loved Rachel, because his love to us is like Jonathan's love to David, 'passing the love of women,' 2 Sam. i. 26.

Thus we have heard what it is that the Lord requires of us, namely, love. Now, let us see what manner of love he requireth, 'Thou shalt love the Lord thy God with all thine heart, with all thy soul, with all thy strength, and with all thy thought.' Here the Lord setteth down the measure of that love which he requireth of us; that, first, it must be true and unfeigned, as proceeding from the heart and mind; secondly, that it must be sound and perfect, 'with all the heart, with all the mind,' &c.

As we must love God *with the heart*, that is, sincerely, so we must love him *with all the heart*, that is, with a perfect love. God is like a jealous husband, loath to have a partner in his love, Exod. xx. 5. He will not have half the heart, nor a piece of the heart, but all the heart. When the heart is divided, it dieth; therefore God will not have the heart divided, lest it die, because he desireth a living, and not a dying heart. He is not like the unkind mother, that would have the child divided, 1 Kings iii. 26, but like the natural mother, who, rather than it should be divided, would forego the child. So God will have all or none; if he may not have all the heart, and all the soul, and all the strength, and all the thought, he will have none at all. The devil, or the world, or the flesh, will play small game, as we use to say, before they will sit out. If they cannot get full possession of our hearts, then they are content to have some part of our love, as it were a little room in our hearts; a wicked thought, or else a consent to sin. Like Pharaoh, the king of Egypt, who, when

he could not keep the Israelites still in bondage,
would keep their wives and children back ; and
when this would not be granted, then he was
content to let them go and do sacrifice ; but their
sheep and their cattle must stay behind ; and when
this might not be obtained, then he desired them
only to bless him before they went, Exod. xii. 32.
But God is of another mind ; he that made all
the hearts of men, and trieth them, and knoweth
them, and reneweth and mollifieth them, and
lighteneth them, and ruleth them, and turneth
them which way it pleaseth him, will have all the
heart, because he hath best right to all. As we
love a ring or a jewel for his sake that gave it,
so we must love all things of this life for his
sake that gave them, and him for his own
sake above all the rest. This perfect love we can
bestow but once, and but one can have it, and
whoso hath it must be our God. If we set our
heart upon riches, we make riches our god ; therefore David saith, Ps. lxii. 10, ' If riches increase,
set not your heart upon them.' If our whole
delight be in eating and drinking, then we make
a god of our belly ; and the apostle tells us,
Philip. iii. 19, that our end is damnation. If we
be given to wantonness and fleshly pleasure, then
Venus is our goddess ; and Solomon tells us,
Prov. vi. 26, that our end will be beggary. But if

we have set our love on God, 'the eye hath not seen, the ear hath not heard, neither hath it entered into the heart of man, what God hath prepared for them that love him,' 1 Cor. ii. 9.

But let us examine the words, 'Thou shalt love thy neighbour as thyself.' Here are four things to be observed : First, what is required, namely, *love* ; secondly, who must love, *thou*, that is, every man ; thirdly, whom we must love, namely, our *neighbour* ; and lastly, how and in what manner we must love him, *as we love ourselves*.

Concerning the first ; as in the former precept, so in this also, the Lord requireth love, wherein he dealeth as a kind father with his children, who is desirous to have them so to resemble him as by their conditions every man may know whose they are. Therefore our loving Father, desirous to have us like himself, requireth us to be kind and loving one to another, as he is kind to the unkind, to the evil, to the just and to the unjust, Mat. v. 45. He will have us perfect as he is perfect, he will have us holy as he is holy, he will have us merciful as he is merciful, he will have us loving as he is love itself.

But let us come to the second thing, which sheweth who is bound to love : *Thou shalt love*. Under this word *thou*, God comprehends every particular man and woman; as if he should say, Thou thyself, and not any other: for ' *Thou* shalt love thy neighbour.' The poor man is not exempted from this precept, because he may love as well as the rich. If he say, I have no wealth, and therefore I cannot shew my love to my neighbour; though he have no wealth, yet he hath a heart, he hath a mind, he has an affection; let him have a loving heart, a loving mind, and a loving affection: if he cannot do well, let him wish well unto his neighbour; if he cannot gratify him with anything that he hath, let him not envy at anything that the rich man hath. For as the rich man shews that he loves his neighbour if he relieves his necessity, so the poor man sheweth that he loves his neighbour if he grieves not at his prosperity. This, therefore, as a general precept, bindeth the poor as well as the rich; it is a common yoke laid upon the neck, and a common burden laid upon the back of every Christian; but yet it is 'an easy yoke, and a light burden,' Mat. xi. 30, because it is love, which maketh all things to seem delightsome. As there are some that would be content to love if they might not give, so there are some that would be content to give if they were sure they should not want; therefore, when it comes to giving, they post it over to their heirs, or to their executors, or to their successors, when they are dead; they are never liberal until they die, and then they are liberal of that which is none of theirs. They think to be excused by the liberality of their heirs; but they are bound to be liberal for themselves; therefore they must not lay the burden upon them, because 'every man must bear his own burden,' Gal. vi. 5.

Now follows the measure of that love which we owe unto our neighbour, expressed in the last words, *as thyself.* Here is the rule whereby our love must be squared, and a most exquisite example of singular love found in ourselves for us to imitate. He saith not, As he loveth thee, or as he is beloved of others, but *as thyself.*

Who knows not how well he loves himself? and therefore who can excuse himself and say, I know not how well I should love my neighbour? But how do we love ourselves? Feignedly, or coldly, or for an hour? I trow not; but truly, and zealously, and every hour. So we must love our neighbour with a true, zealous, and a constant love. We must not pass by, as the priest and the Levite; but pour our oil into their wounds, with the Samaritan, to help, to relieve them and comfort them. We must love our neighbour though he be envious, as David loved Saul, requiting good for evil; and as Joseph loved

Potiphar, not enticed to sin against him. 'Love is the fulfilling of the law.' Now we are come to the answer of Christ unto the lawyer's question. The question was, 'What must be done to inherit eternal life?' The answer is, Do that which thou hast said, that is, Love God above all, and thy neighbour as thyself; and thou shalt live, thou shalt inherit eternal life.

But here some man may object and say, Is any man able to do this that God requireth? and if he be not, why then doth God command us that which we cannot perform? Herein almighty God deals with us as a father dealeth with his children. If a man have a son of seven years of age, he will furnish him with bow and arrows, and lead him into the fields; set him to shoot at a mark that is twelve score off, promising to give him some goodly thing if he hits the mark; and though the father know the child cannot shoot so far, yet will he have him aim at a mark beyond his reach, thereby to try the strength and for-wardness of his child; and though he shoot short, yet the father will encourage him. Even so almighty God hath furnished us with judgment and reason, as it were with certain artillery, where-by we are able to distinguish between good and evil, and sent us into the world, as it were into the open fields, and set his law before us as a

174

mark, as David speaks, promising to give us the
kingdom of heaven if we hit the same ; and
albeit he knoweth that we cannot hit this mark,
that is, keep the law which he hath set before us,
yet, for the exercise of our faith, and for the
testifying of our duty and obedience towards him,
he will always have us be aiming at it ; and though
we come short of that duty and obedience which he
requireth at our hands, yet doth he accept and
reward our good endeavour ; but if we stubbornly
refuse to frame ourselves after his will, then may
he justly be angry and displeased with us.
Therefore, though thou canst not perfectly keep
the law of God, yet if thou endeavour thyself to
the utmost of thy power to observe the same,
the Lord, that 'worketh in us both the will and
the work,' will accept the will for the work ; and
that which is wanting in us, he will supply with
his own righteousness.

THE SWEET SONG OF OLD
FATHER SIMEON

*Lord, now lettest thou thy servant depart in peace,
according to thy word. For mine eyes have
seen thy salvation, which thou hast prepared
before the face of all people; a light to be
revealed to the Gentiles, and the glory of thy
people Israel.*—Luke ii. 29–32.

THIS is the sweet song of old father Simeon,
wherein is set forth the joyful and peaceable
death of the righteous, after that they have
embraced Christ Jesus with heart and mind
unfeignedly, as he did, seeing their death is to be
the beginning of a better and more joyful and
pleasant life than the former.

But before we proceed farther in it, let us
hear a little of that which went before. The
evangelist saith, ver. 25, &c., 'And, behold, there
was a man in Jerusalem, whose name was Simeon;
this man was just, and feared God, and waited
for the consolation of Israel, and the Holy Ghost
was upon him. And a revelation,' &c.

Simeon feared God. Religion may well be called fear, for there is no religion where fear is wanting; for 'the fear of the Lord is the beginning of wisdom,' Prov. i. 7. And this privilege hath God given to those that fear him, that they need to fear nothing else.

And waited for the consolation of Israel. Simeon also waited for the consolation of Israel, until he had embraced in his arms him whom he so long longed to see and feel. How many waiters be there in the world! yet few wait as Simeon did; but some wait for honour, some for riches, some for pleasures, some for ease, some for rewards, some for money, some for a dear year, and some for a golden day, as they call it; but Simeon waited, and expected with many a long look, until he had seen and embraced Christ Jesus, the light of the Gentiles, the glory of Israel, the salvation of all that with a faithful and zealous affection and love do wait for his coming, to the comfort of the afflicted, and to the terrifying of the wicked and ungodly, which have not already waited, neither embraced him, as Simeon did.

And waited for the consolation of Israel. Faith in all afflictions doth lift up her head, waiting in assured hope beyond all hope; and seeing the clouds scattered over her head, yet she is ever comfortable to herself, saying, Anon it will be calm ; and although all the friends in the world do fail, yet it never faileth nor fainteth, but even keepeth promise in that which by the verity of the Spirit of God it assureth, until her joy be fulfilled.

And when the parents brought in the child Jesus to do for him according to the customs of the law, then he took him in his arms. Happy Simeon embracing Christ ; but not happy that he embraced him with his hands ; but therefore happy, because he embraced him in heart. ' Happy are the eyes and blessed which see the things that ye see, and the ears that hear the things that ye hear,' saith Christ, Mat. xiii. 16 ; but cursed are we that hearing and seeing do not repent ; for we cannot be blessed by hearing and seeing only, unless we hear and see with profit, so that we in heart embrace Christ. But we will object that we are Israelites, and are circumcised, and have received the sacrament of Christ's blood, that we might be his people, and he our God. But this will not excuse us, nor make us seem anything better in the sight of God, but rather worse, if we have not ceased to embrace the world, to embrace vanities, and have not unfeignedly embraced the word of God, and also the Lord Jesus Christ. For it is said, that Christ ' came amongst his own, and his own received him not,' John i. 11 ; but therefore

178

accursed are so many of them as reject their own salvation, which being freely offered unto them, they will not stretch forth their hands to receive it ; that is, will not attend with their ears to hear it, or at least will not enlarge their hearts to embrace it.

Simeon praised God. Simeon was thankful. Here is the example, but where be they that follow it ? If nine lepers be cleansed, yet but one returneth to give thanks ; then one is all. Unthankfulness is the first guest that sitteth at the table ; for some will not stick to say, that they never said grace since they were children ; but if they had said, they never had grace since they were children, I would rather believe them. Do you not say, 'Give us this day our daily bread '? If you do, for shame say so no more, beg no more at God's hands, until you be more thankful for that you have received.

Lord, now lettest thou thy servant depart. Simeon waiting for the consolation of Israel, longing to see the Saviour, was like the hart panting for the waterbrooks, till he had beheld his best beloved ; but as soon as he had taken him in his arms whom his soul desired to see, he so thirsted for death, that he thenceforth thought of, sought after, besought God for, nothing, but to leave this life, and hence to depart ; for he forthwith, singing,

prayed, ' Now lettest thou thy servant depart.'
But do you, say some, commend him herein? did
he well? May not any man desire death? May
not the fastened ship in a strange land desire to
be loosed, to hasten to his longed-for port at
home? May not a man imprisoned amongst bitter
enemies desire to be set at liberty, to return to his
own country, in freedom to live amongst his sweet
friends? Are we not strangers here, and by
unpeaceable, most deadly enemies, our own flesh,
the world, and the devil, held prisoners in the
chains of sin and manifold infirmities? and is
not our home heaven, and the saints and angels
our most dear friends? No marvel, then, that
Simeon here desireth to be loosed, or let depart.
And Paul professeth he desireth to be dissolved,
Philip. i. 23, or unloosed, as ships in a strange
land fastened, as strangers amongst cruel enemies
imprisoned. They were unnatural if they did not;
it were unreasonable to require they should not;
for we not only may think it lawful, but must also
acknowledge it even a necessary duty, to desire
death. For is there till then in us any perfect,
yea, any pure obedience of God? Doth not sin,
as long as this life lasteth, dwell in our members?
Is there any passage to the perfect life but by the
first death? The fish which is taken in the net
out of the sea struggleth to get in again; and

Adam, thrust out of paradise, would fain have
been within again : how much more should we be
desirous to be settled in the new paradise, in
assurance never to be put from thence? Therefore
also it is not only our duty to desire death, but
also as soon as any clearly seeth Christ, presently
he desireth to die. For though his state be never
so pleasant, though his life be most delightful,
though he excel in riches, and pleasures, and
honours, and knowledge, and glory, and far
exceed all that ever were ; yet at the sight of
Christ he even rejoiceth to forego all ; the love
of the world falling away like the mantle of Elias,
when he was rapt into heaven ; and so crieth with
the apostle, 'I desire to be dissolved,' that he
may be with Christ. For Christ is light, and as
soon as they see him, they see also themselves,
and the world's false happiness ; his glory, and
their shame and filthiness, which maketh them
wish for death, that they may cease to sin against
God, and perfectly please him, and enjoy true
happiness with him ; for all sin is blood in their
eyes, and all worldly pleasures vanities.

None but the truly righteous, none but they
that by faith are assured they are before God
righteous, can rightly desire death. For who
would desire a change but for the better? But
all that are ignorant of God, all the unfaithful,

what knowledge soever they have, cannot be in better ease dead than they are now in living, though most miserably pained ; nay, they cannot be without just fear, when they forego this life, to feel for ever the second death. But the faithful, having their consciences quiet, and also joyful in Christ, free from the fear of that death they have deserved, and assured by death to pass to that life which God to all the faithful hath promised, earnestly wish to die, in all fervent love of God, and zeal of his glory, that so they may cease from offending their good God, and never cease magnifying his mercy ; shewing thereby that they are weary of the service and bondage of Satan and sin, and assured after death to enjoy the true life, most fully glorifying God, and most perfectly pleasing him for ever; and therefore also they desire death, not shortening their life, but waiting his leisure and calling, thereby glorifying God, as in their lives they have done and sought to do.

For man was not born at his own will, and therefore may not die at his own pleasure. Therefore they beg it of God, referring themselves ever to his good will, when, where, and how by death they shall glorify him, still desiring it, but never wilfully procuring it.

Have seen, &c. O Lord, saith he, I desire now to be dissolved and free from the bondage of sin, which so long hath inhabited in my mortal body ; for now he is come by whom thou hast promised to free us and set us at liberty ; he is come by whom thou hast promised to break the serpent's head ; and he is come that will heal our infirmities, and give strength against sin and Satan, by faith and peace towards God, through love. And now, saith he, I have embraced him, and thankfully do receive him. I believe and am persuaded that this is the same Messiah whom the Father promised, and the prophets foretold, all Israel longed for and expected, who is the light of the Gentiles, the glory of Israel, and the God of the whole world. So they which love the truth of God, and wait with desire to be fulfilled with the knowledge thereof, such shall not die until they have their hearts' desire with contemplation thereof.

Have seen thy, &c. There be many sights of Christ ; all go not up to the mount, as Peter, James and John, Mat. xvii. 1 : all see not his face, with Moses, Exod. xxxiii. ; all sleep not in his lap, with John, John xiii. 23, xxi. 20 ; all are not taken up into heaven, like Paul, 2 Cor. xii. 2 ; all embrace him not in their arms, with Simeon. But as pleaseth God, so he sheweth himself unto us ; and all that love him, both see him and embrace him.

183

To some he shews himself as in a glass, to some generally, to some particularly; some he calleth early, and some he calleth late; and there is no hour in the day wherein he calleth not some to go labour in his vineyard, Mat. xx. To some he sheweth himself by angels, and to other some by visions. Abraham saw three angels, Gen. xviii. 2, Lot saw but two, Gen. xix. 1, Manoah's wife saw but one, Judges xiii. 3; and yet one was enough. It is said that Abraham saw Christ's days, John viii. 56; but we see him clearer than Abraham, and clearer than John, if we believe in him as we should. Some see Christ, and not his salvation; and some see his salvation, and do not embrace it. We see Christ when we hear his word, and we embrace his salvation when we believe it; they see him that hear him, they embrace him that follow him. But how can they believe the word of God which hear it not? how can they embrace Christ which know him not? and all through ignorance, having not the means to see him, because their leaders are either blind guides, sleepy watchmen, or hireling shepherds.

Thy salvation. He came not by angels, or by men, or by any other means, but only from the alone and eternal God. He calleth him 'thy salvation'; for his name was not given him by Joseph, nor by Mary, but by the angel of God,

Luke i. 31, signifying that he was come from heaven. The Father saw him when he was born, the Spirit came upon him when he was baptized, the angels ministered unto him in the wilderness, his enemies subscribed unto him upon the cross, the virgin travailed, the star walked, the wise men came out of far countries to worship him. Then is not this Jehovah, the mighty God, whose birth is glorious, whose life is famous, whose death is meritorious?

Thy salvation. The only Saviour is here called *salvation* itself; for if he were called a bare Saviour only, then you might likely understand by him some other saviour; but here he is called salvation itself, to shew that there is no other. For there be more saviours, but no more salvations; as there be many ways to death, and yet but one death. The brazen serpent was a figure of Christ, Num. xxi., John iii. 14, 15, that they which are stung by sin, by fire, and by the serpent which beguiled Eve, may make speed, because there is no remedy but to come to Christ.

Salvation is born; therefore we were all in the state of condemnation before. Light is come; therefore we sat all in darkness before. Glory is come; therefore we were all loaden with shame before. Life is come; to shew that we were all dead in sin before. Life is come, and light, and

185

salvation ; life to the dead, light to the blind, and salvation to the damned. For Christ is called *salvation*, to shew that without him we are all damned, fire-brands of hell, heirs of condemnation, and forsaken of God. To him that is sick, it is easy to be thankful when he is whole ; but when he is whole, it is harder to be thankful than to be sick.

Thy salvation. This word salvation is a sweet word, yea, the sweetest word in all the Scripture ; and yet many despise this worthy jewel, because they know not what it is worth ; like the daws, which would rather have a barley-corn than a pearl or a jewel, because they know not the value thereof.

'O Lord, what is man, that thou art so mindful of him?' Ps. viii. 4. O man, what is God, that thou art so unmindful of him? If a friend had given us anything, we would have thanked him heartily for it ; but to him that hath given us all things, we will not give so much as thanks. Now, therefore, let the rock gush out water again, and let our stony hearts pour forth streams of tears in unfeigned repentance. We have all called upon you, but none regardeth us ; as though God were as Baal, and as though Dives felt no pain, nor Lazarus joy, but all were forgotten. Many times Christ cometh into the temple, and there is scarce a Simeon to embrace him. The babe is here, but where is Simeon?

If God had not loved us better than we loved ourselves, we should have perished long ere this; and yet we embrace not Christ, as Simeon, who hath saved us from temporal and spiritual punishment. We are invited to a banquet; he who calleth us to it is God. What is the banquet? Salvation. Who are the guests? The angels and the saints. What is the fare? Joy, peace, righteousness. This is the fare, and we invite you every one; yet who will come at our bidding? Some for want of faith, some for want of love, some for want of knowledge, have despised his holy banquet; yet unto this art thou called still, O soul unworthy to be beloved.

Which thou hast prepared before the face of all people, &c. He speaks this to the end that the eyes of all mankind may be fixed upon him, as the eyes of all Israel were fixed upon the brazen serpent in the wilderness, Num. xxi.; and when they be stinged with the sting of that fiery serpent which deceived our forefathers, they may fly unto him for help, lest they perish in their sin, and their blood be on their own heads.

Which thou hast prepared. He was prepared long ago, as it doth most plainly appear; for the virgin which bare him, the place of his birth, the poor state wherein he was, his miracles, his apostles, his torments, his cross, his death, his resurrection and ascension into heaven, all these were foreshewed and foretold long before they came to pass. Therefore some said, Who is this that is so often spoken of by the prophets? Who is this that can do many miracles that the scribes and pharisees cannot do? that can raise the dead, that can cease the winds, that can calm the waters, at whose suffering the earth quaked, the sun hid his face, darkness came over all, and who, being dead, rose again by his own power, and ascended into heaven in the sight of a great multitude? How can it be then but it must be known ' before the face of all people,' which was so manifest by dreams, by visions, by oracles, by power, by authority, and everything? For there was nothing which had not a tongue to speak for God. Everything was prepared for him before he came to be revealed. He came not in the beginning nor in the ending. He came not in the ending, that we which come after him might long for his second coming. He came not in the beginning, because that such a Prince as he should have many banners and triumphs before him. He came not in the beginning, because the eyes of faith should not be dazzled in him, and lest they which should live in the latter times should forget him and his coming, which was so long before ; even as you forget that which I have said as soon as you are gone hence. He came not in the beginning, because if he had come before man had sinned, man would have acknowledged no need of a physician ; but he came when man had sinned, and had felt the smart of sin. For when they were cast out of paradise, they ran unto Christ, as the Israelites did to the serpent. He came not in the beginning, but in the perfect age of the world, to shew that he brought with him perfection, perfect joy, perfect peace, perfect wisdom, perfect righteousness, perfect justice, perfect truth ; signifying thereby, that notwithstanding he came in the perfect age thereof, yet he found all things imperfect.

If you love joy and gladness, Christ is joy and gladness ; if you love comfort, why, Christ is the comfort of all that bear his cross ; if you love life, Christ is eternal life ; if you love peace, Christ is peace ; if you love riches, Christ is full of heavenly riches, and full of liberality, to bestow them upon all such as love God. So Christ is all in all unto the godly, and they have more joy in Christ always, and in all things, than the richest and most glorious and sumptuous prince in the world, than Solomon himself had in worldly riches, honours, pleasures, joy, ease, or felicity. For the wicked, which put their trust in riches, and make them gods of gold and money, of ease and pleasures, though they do all that they can to fulfil their lusts, and take never so much pleasure, and be never so merry, yet they can have no true joy, nor peace of conscience ; for all the peace, the mirth and sport they have is but deceit, all false and undurable, like the grass, green in the morning, and withered ere night. So then we see, that perfect joy can be had in nothing but in God and in Jesus Christ. Wherefore, as by the stream you may be led to the fountain ; even so let the joy and peace of this life serve to lead us to God, who is perfect joy and peace ; and there let us rest, like the wise men, which were guided by the star to come to the true Son of grace, Jesus Christ, when he was born. And if we rest not in him when we have found him, there is no rest for us ; we shall be like the restless dove, which fluttered about, and found no rest any way till she returned to the ark.

To be revealed. Have an eye to the future tense ; that which is not, shall be. As for example, Solomon *was* wise, but he *is* foolish ; Samson *was* strong, but he *is* weak ; Judas *was* a preacher, but he *is* a traitor ; Paul *was* a persecutor, but he *is* a preacher ; Peter *was* a denier of Christ, but now he *is* a bold professor of Christ ; Moses *was*

learned in the wisdom of the Egyptians, but now
he *is* learned in the wisdom of God, by which the
wisdom of the Egyptians is made but mere foolishness in the sight of God. Others, as heathen
philosophers, Plato, Aristotle, Cato, Crates, and
such like, were counted very wise men in the sight
of the world; yea, they wrote so many books
full of wisdom, and also adorned with notable
sentences and witty sayings, that one would think
all wisdom were buried with them, so famous
were they, and so full of earthly understanding,
teaching manners, counsels, and policies. Yet,
for my part, I have neither seen nor heard of any
such being wise in worldly things, and without the
wisdom of God, but that they have committed
some notorious foolishness in the sight of all men.
For if your wisdom consist in eloquence of words,
in profundity of wit, to gain craftily and spend
warily, to invent laws, to expound riddles, and
interpret dreams, to tell fortunes, and prophesy
of matters by learning, all your wisdom is but
vexation of the spirit; for all these, without the
fear of God, do us no more good than their wit
did these philosophers, which notwithstanding sat
in darkness.

What then is to be done? As Jacob said to
his wives and children, Give me your idols, that
I may bury them, Gen. xxxv.; so say I unto you,

Give me your superstitions, that I may bury them,
that they may remain with you or in you no longer,
to the dishonour of God, offending of your weak
brethren, or to my grief. For I am jealous over
you ; and because you are mine, and I am yours,
oh that my voice were as the whirlwind, to beat
down, root out, and blow away all your superstitions, that they may no longer reign amongst
you ! Or rather, oh that Christ, which is our light,
were come into us all, and shined so bright, that
we were ashamed of all our darkness ; of all, not
of mind only, but of will also, and of works, that
we no longer would walk in darkness.

THE BENEFIT OF CONTENTATION

*Godliness is great gain, if a man be content
with that he hath.*—1 Tim. vi. 6.

BECAUSE when we preach, we know not
whether we shall preach again, my care is, to choose
fit and proper texts, to speak that which I would
speak, and that which is necessary for you to
hear. Therefore, thinking with myself what
doctrine were fittest for you, I sought for a text
which speaks against covetousness, which I may
call the Londoners' sin. Although God hath
given you more than others, which should turn
covetousness into thankfulness, yet as the ivy
groweth with the oak, so covetousness hath grown
with riches ; every man wisheth the philosopher's
stone ; and who is within these walls that thinks
he hath enough, though there be so many that
have too much ? As the Israelites murmured as
much when they had manna, as when they were
without it, Exod. xvi. 2, Num. xi. 4 ; so they
which have riches covet as much as they which
are without them ; that conferring your minds

and your wealth together, I may truly say, this city is rich, if it were not covetous. This is the devil which bewitcheth you, to think that you have not enough, when you have more than you need. If you cannot choose but covet riches, I will shew you riches which you may covet: 'Godliness is great riches.' In which words, as Jacob craved of his wives and his servants to give him their idols, that he might bury them, Gen. xxxv. 4 ; so Paul craveth your covetousness, that he might bury it ; and that ye might be no losers, he offereth you the vantage ; instead of gain, he proposeth great gain. 'Godliness is great gain'; as if he should say, will you covet little gain before great ? You have found little joy in money, you shall find great joy in the Holy Ghost ; you have found little peace in the world, you shall find great peace in conscience. Thus seeing the world strive for the world, like beggars thrusting at a dole, lawyer against lawyer, brother against brother, neighbour against neighbour, for the golden apple, that poor Naboth cannot hold his own, because so many Ahabs are sick for his vineyard, 1 Kings xxi. 4 ; when he had found the disease, like a skilful physician, he goeth about to pick out the greedy worm which maketh men so hungry, and setteth such a glass before them that will make a shilling seem as great as a pound, a cottage seem as fair as a palace, and a plough seem as goodly as a diadem; that he which hath but twenty pounds, shall be as merry as he which hath an hundred; and he which hath an hundred, shall be as jocund as he which hath a thousand; and he which hath a thousand, shall be as well contented as he which hath a million.

He will not only prove godliness to be *gain*, but *great gain*; as if he should say, more gainful than your wares, and rents, and fines, and interests, as though he would make the lawyer, and merchant, and mercer, and draper, and patron, and landlord, and all the men of riches believe, that godliness will make them rich sooner than covetousness.

He was not content to call godliness *gain*, but he calleth it *great gain*; as if he would say, *gain*, and more than *gain*; riches, and better than riches; a kingdom, and greater than a kingdom. As when the prophets would distinguish between the idol-gods and the living God, they call him the great God; so the gain of godliness is called great gain. The riches of the world are called earthly, transitory, snares, thorns, dung, as though they were not worthy to be counted riches; and therefore, to draw the earnest love of men from them, the Holy Ghost brings them in with these names of disdain, to disgrace them with their loves; but when he comes to godliness, which is the riches of the soul, he calleth it great riches, heavenly riches, unsearchable riches, everlasting riches, with all the names of honour, and all the names of pleasure, and all the names of happiness. As a woman trims and decks herself with an hundred ornaments, only to make her amiable, so the Holy Ghost setteth out godliness with names of honour, and names of pleasure, and names of happiness, as it were in her jewels, with letters of commendation to make her be beloved. Lest any riches should compare with godliness, he gives it a name above others, and calleth it great riches, as if he would make a distinction between riches and riches, between the gain of covetousness and the gain of godliness, the peace of the world and the peace of conscience, the joy of riches and the joy of the Holy Ghost. The worldly men have a kind of peace, and joy, and riches. But I cannot call it *great*, because they have not enough, they are not contented as the godly are; therefore only godliness hath this honour, to be called *great riches*. The gain of covetousness is nothing but wealth; but the gain of godliness is wealth, and peace, and joy, and love of God, and the remission of sins, and everlasting life. Therefore only godliness hath this honour, to be called great gain. Riches makes bate, but godliness makes peace ; riches breeds covetousness, but godliness brings contentation ; riches makes men unwilling to die, but godliness makes men ready to die ; riches often hurt the owner, but godliness profiteth the owner and others. Therefore, only godliness hath this honour, to be called great riches.

Thus every labour hath an end, but covetousness hath none ; like a suitor in law, which thinks to have an end this term, and that term, and the lawyer which should procure his peace, prolongeth his strife, because he hath an action to his purse, as his adversary hath to his land ; so he which is set on coveting, doth drink brine, which makes him thirst more, and sees no haven till he arrive at death ; when he hath lied, he is ready to lie again ; when he hath sworn, he is ready to swear again ; when he hath deceived, he is ready to deceive again ; when the day is past, he would it were to begin again ; when the term is ended, he wisheth it were to come again ; and though his house be full, and his shop full, and his coffers full, and his purse full, yet his heart is not full, but lank and empty, like the disease which we call the wolf, that is always eating, and yet keeps the body lean. The ant

197

doth eat the food which he findeth ; the lion doth refresh himself with the prey that he taketh, but the covetous man lieth by his money, as a sick man sits by his meat, and hath no power to taste it, but to look upon it ; like the prince to whom Elisha said, that he should 'see the corn with his eyes, but none should come within his mouth,' 2 Kings vii. 22. Thus the covetous man makes a fool of himself. He coveteth to covet ; he gathereth to gather ; he laboureth to labour ; he careth to care ; as though his office were to fill a coffer full of angels, and then to die like an ass, which carrieth treasure on his back all day, and at night they are taken from him, which did him no good but load him. How happy were some, if they knew not gold from lead ? 'If thou be wise,' saith Solomon, 'thou shalt be wise for thyself,' Prov. ix. 12. But he which is covetous, is covetous against himself. For what a plague is this, unless one would kill himself, for a man to spend all his life in carking, and pining, and scraping, as though he should do nothing but gather in this world, to spend in the next, unless he be sure that he should come again when he is dead, to eat those scraps which he hath gotten with all his stir ? Therefore covetousness may well be called *misery*, and the covetous *miserable*, for they are miserable indeed.

When the law is ended, if the man be not content, he is in trouble still; when his disease is cured, if he be not content, he is sick still; when his want is supplied, if he be not content, he is in want still; when bondage is turned into liberty, if he be not content, he is in bondage still; but though he be in law, and sickness, and poverty, and bondage, yet, if he be content, he is free, and rich, and merry, and quiet, even as Adam was warm though he had no clothes, Gen. ii. 25.

Such a commander is contentation, that wheresoever she setteth foot, an hundred blessings wait upon her; in every disease she is a physician, in every strife she is a lawyer, in every doubt she is a preacher, in every grief she is a comforter, like a sweet perfume, which taketh away the evil scent, and leaveth a pleasant scent for it. As the unicorn's horn dipped in the fountain makes the waters which were corrupt and noisome clear and wholesome upon the sudden, so, whatsoever estate godliness comes unto, it saith like the apostles, 'Peace be to this house,' Luke x. 5, peace be to this heart, peace be to this man.

I may liken it to the five loaves and two fishes, wherewith Christ fed five thousand persons, and yet there were twelve baskets full of that which was left, which could not fill one basket when it

was whole. Thus their little feast was made a
great feast ; so the godly, though they have but
little for themselves, yet they have something for
others, like the widow's mite, Matt. xii. 41 ; that
they may say as the disciples said to Christ, they
want nothing, though they have nothing, Luke
xxii. 35. Contentation wanteth nothing, and a
good heart is worth all. For if she want bread,
she can say as Christ said, 'I have another bread,'
John iv. 32 ; if she want riches, she can say, I
have other riches ; if she want strength, she can
say, I have other strength; if she want friends, she
can say, I have other friends. Thus the godly find
all within that they seek without. Therefore, if
you see a man contented with that he hath, it is
a great sign that godliness is entered into him,
for the heart of man was made a temple for God,
and nothing can fill it but God alone. Therefore
Paul saith after his conversion, that which he
could never say before his conversion, 'I have
learned to be content,' Philip. iv. 12. First he
learned godliness, then godliness taught him contentation. Now (saith Paul), 'I have learned to
be content'; as though this were a lesson for
every Christian to learn, to be content.

When the churl's barns were full, he bade his
soul take rest, thinking to gain rest by covetousness, that he might say, Riches gain rest, as well

as godliness ; but see what happened : that night when he began to take his rest, riches, and rest, and soul, and all, were taken from him, Luke xii. 16. Did he not gain fair ? Would he have taken such pains if he had thought of such rest ? Covetousness may gain riches, but it cannot gain rest ; ye may think like this churl, to rest when your barns, and shops, and coffers are full ; but ye shall find it true which Isaiah saith, 'There is no rest to the ungodly,' Isa. xlviii. 22 ; therefore the wise man, to prevent all hope of rest, or honour, or profit by sin, speaks as though he had tried, 'A man cannot be established by iniquity,' Prov. xii. 3. Therefore he cannot be quieted, nor satisfied by the gain of deceit, or bribes, or lies, or usury, which is iniquity. Therefore blessed is the man whom godliness doth make rich ; 'for when the blessing of the Lord maketh rich,' saith Solomon, 'he doth add no sorrow to it' ; but, saith he, 'the revenue of the wicked is trouble,' as though his money were care. Wherefore let patron, and landlord, and lawyer, and all, say now, that Paul hath chosen the better riches, 'which thief, nor moth, nor canker can corrupt' ; these are the riches at last, that we must dwell with, when all the rest which we have lied for, and sworn for, and fretted for, and cozened for, and broken our sleep for, and lost many sermons for, forsake us, like servants which change their masters ; then godliness shall seem as great gain to us as it did to Paul ; and he which loved the world most, would give all that he hath for a dram of faith, that he might be sure to go to heaven, when he is dead, though he went towards hell so long as he lived.

Therefore what counsel shall I give you, but as Christ counselled his disciples, Be not friends to riches, but 'make you friends of riches'; and know this, that if ye cannot say as Paul saith, 'I have learned to be content,' Philip. iv. 12, godliness is not yet come to your house ; for the companion of godliness is contentation ; which, when she comes, will bring you all things. Therefore as Christ saith, ' If the Son make you free, you shall be free indeed,' John vii. 36 ; so I say, if godliness make ye rich, ye shall be rich indeed. The Lord Jesus make ye doers of that ye have heard. Amen.

THE AFFINITY OF THE FAITHFUL

Then came to him his mother and brethren, and
could not come near him for the press. And
it was told him by certain which said, Thy
mother and brethren stand without and would
see thee. But he answered and said unto
them, My mother and brethren are those
which hear the word of God, and do it.—
Luke viii. 19–21.

HERE is Christ preaching, a great press
hearing, his mother and his friends interrupting,
and Christ again withstanding the interruption,
with a comfortable doctrine of his mercies towards
them which hear the word of God and do it.
When Christ was about a work, and many were
gathered together to hear him, the devil thought
with himself, as the priests and Sadducees did in
the fourth of the Acts : If I let him alone thus, all
the world will follow him, and I shall be like
Rachel, without children ; therefore, devising the
likeliest policy to frustrate and disgrace but one
of his sermons, thereby to make the people

unwilling to hear him again, as he set Eve upon Adam, Gen. iii. 6, and made Job's wife his instrument, Job ii. 9, when he could not fit it himself; so he sendeth Christ's mother, and putteth in the minds of his kinsmen, to come unto him at that instant, when he was in this holy exercise, and call upon him while he was preaching, to come away, and go with them. Christ seeing the serpent's dealing, how he made his mother the tempter, that all the auditory might go away empty, and say where they came, We heard the man which is called Jesus, and he began to preach unto us, with such words, as though he would carry us to heaven; but in the midst of his sermon came his mother and brethren to him, that it might be known what a kinsman they had; and so soon as he heard that they were come, suddenly he brake off his sermon, and slipped away from us, to go and make merry with them. Christ, I say, seeing this train laid by Satan, to disgrace him (as he doth all his ministers), did not leave off speaking, as they thought he would; but as if God had appointed all this to credit and renown him, that which was noised here to interrupt his doctrine, he taketh for an occasion to teach another doctrine, that there is a nearer conjunction between Christ and the faithful, than between the mother and the son,

which are one flesh. Therefore when they say,
'Thy mother and brethren are come to speak with
thee,' he pointeth to his hearers and saith, ' These
are my mother and brethren which hear the word
of God and do it.'

Note, that in holy Scripture there be four
sorts of brethren : brethren by nature, so Esau
and Jacob are called brethren, Gen. xxvii. 30,
because they had one father and one mother ;
brethren by nation, so all the Jews are called
brethren, Deut. xv. 1, because they were of one
country ; brethren by consanguinity, so all are
called brethren which are of one family, and
so Abraham called Lot his brother, Gen. xiii. 8,
and Sarah his sister, Gen. xii. 13, because they
were of one line ; brethren by profession, so all
Christians are called brethren, Mat. xxiii., because
they are of one religion. These are brethren of
the third order, that is, of consanguinity, because
they were of one family.

Now, when his mother and his brethren were
come to see him, it is said, that they could not
come near him for the press. Here were auditors
enough. Christ so flowed now with his disciples,
that his mother could have no room to hear
him ; but after a while it was low water again.
When the shepherd was strucken, the sheep were
scattered, Mat. xxvi. 31 ; when he preached in

205

the streets, and the temples, and the fields, then many flocked after him ; but when he preached upon the cross, then they left him which said they would never forsake him ; then there was a great press to see him die, as there was here to hear him preach. And many of these which seemed like brethren and sisters, were his betrayers, and accusers, and persecutors, Mat. xxvii. ; so inconstant are we in our zeal, more than in anything else. Thus much of their coming and calling to Christ. Now, to the doctrine which lieth in it.

Here be two speakers : one saith, ' Thy mother and thy brethren are come to speak unto thee ' ; the other saith, ' Those are my mother and brethren which hear the word of God and do it.' The scope of the evangelist is this : first, that Christ would not hinder his doctrine for mother, or brethren, or any kinsman ; then, to shew that there is a nearer conjunction between Christ and the faithful, than the mother and the son. The first is written for our comfort ; touching the first, he which teacheth us to honour our father and mother, Exod. xx., doth not teach here to contemn father and mother, because he speaks of another mother, for it is said, that ' he was obedient to his parents.' This he sheweth, when, being found in the temple amongst the doctors, he left all, to go with his mother, because she sought him ; so he honoured her, that he left all for her, Luke ii. 46. This he shewed again at his death ; being upon the cross, he was not unmindful of her, for pointing unto John, he said, ' Mother, behold thy son '; and pointing unto her, he said, ' Behold thy mother,' John xix. 26.

Three things children receive of their parents, life, maintenance, and instruction. For these three they owe other three ; for life, they owe love ; for maintenance, they owe obedience ; for instruction, they owe reverence. For life, they must be loved as fathers ; for maintenance, they must be obeyed as masters ; for instruction, they must be reverenced as tutors. But as there is a King of kings, which must be obeyed above kings, so there is a Father of fathers, which must be obeyed above fathers ; therefore sometimes you must answer like the son, when he was bid to go into his father's vineyard, ' I will go '; and sometimes you must answer as Christ answered, ' I must go about my Father's business.'

When two milch kine did carry the ark of the Lord to Bethshemesh, their calves were shut up at home, 1 Sam. vi. 10, because the kine should not stay, when they heard their calves cry after them ; so when thou goest about the Lord's business, thou shalt hear a cry of thy father, and thy mother, and thy brethren, and thy sisters, and thy kindred, to stay thee, but then thou must think of another Father, as Christ thought of another mother; and so, as those kine went on till the Lord brought them where the ark should rest, so thou shalt go on till the Lord bring thee where thou shalt have rest. It is better to fly from our friends, as Abraham did, Gen. xi. 3, and xii. 11, than to stay with some friends, as Samson did with Delilah, Judges xvi. 14, &c.

I may say, Beware of kinsmen, as well as our Saviour said, Beware of men, for this respect of cousinage made Eli his sons priests, 1 Sam. ii.; and this respect of cousinage hath made many like priests in England. This respect of cousinage hath made Samuel's sons Judges, 1 Sam. viii. 1; and this respect of cousinage hath made many like judges in England. This respect of cousinage brought Tobias into the Levites' chamber, Neh. xiii. 4, 5; and this respect of cousinage hath brought many gentlemen into preachers' livings, which will not out again. As Christ preferred his spiritual kinsmen, so we prefer our earthly kinsmen. Many privileges, many offices, and many benefices, have stooped to this voice, Thy mother calleth thee, or, Thy kinsmen would have thee. As this voice came to Christ while he was labouring, so many such voices come to us while

we are labouring. One saith, Pleasure would
speak with you ; another saith, Profit would speak
with you ; another saith, Ease would speak with
you ; another saith, A deanery would speak with
you ; another saith, A bishopric would speak
with you ; another saith, The court would speak
with you.

Here is a genealogy of Christ, which Matthew
and Luke never spake of. As Christ saith, ' I
have another bread which you know not ' ; so he
saith, I have other kinsmen which you know not.

St John, writing to a lady which brought up
her children in the fear of God, calleth her ' the
elect lady,' 2 John 1, shewing that the chiefest
honour of ladies, and lords, and princes, is to be
elect of God. St Luke, speaking of certain
Bereans, which received the word of God with
love, calls them ' more noble men than the rest,'
Acts xvii. 11, shewing, that God counteth none
noble but such as are of a noble spirit. As John
calleth none elect but the virtuous ; and Luke
calleth none noble but the religious ; so Christ
calleth none his kinsmen but the righteous ; and
of those only he saith, ' These are my mother and
my brethren, which hear the word of God and
do it.'

Now for this love. Christ calls them by
all the names of love ; his father, and his brethren,

and his sisters. In Rom. vi. they are called his
servants; if that be not enough, in John xv. they
are called his friends; if that be not enough, in
Luke xxiv. they are called his brethren; if that be
not enough, in Mark i. they are called his children;
if that be not enough, here they are called his
mother; if that be not enough, in Canticles the
5th they are called his spouse, to shew that he
loveth them with all love; the mother's love, the
brother's love, the sister's love, the master's love,
and the friend's love.

If all these loves could be put together, yet
Christ's love exceedeth them all; and the mother,
and the brother, and the sister, and the child, and
the kinsman, and the friend, and the servant,
would not do and suffer so much among them all,
as Christ hath done and suffered for us alone.
Such a love we kindle in Christ, when we hear
his word, and do it, that we are as dear unto him
as all his kindred together.

Now as we are his mother, so should we carry
him in our hearts, as his mother did in her arms.
As we are his brethren, so we should prefer him,
as Joseph did Benjamin, Gen. xliii. 34. As we
are his spouse, so we should embrace him, as
Isaac did Rebekah; if thou be a kinsman, do like
a kinsman.

Now we come to the marks of these kinsmen,

which I may call the arms of his house. As Christ saith, 'By this all men shall know my disciples, if they love one another'; so he saith, By this shall all men know my kinsmen, if they 'hear the word of God, and do it.'

As there is a kindred by the father's side, and a kindred by the mother's side, so there is a kindred of hearers, and a kindred of doers. In Matthew it is said, 'He which heareth the will of my Father, and doth it'; here it is said, 'He which heareth the word of God, and doth it'; both are one, for his word is his will, and therefore it is called his will, Ps. cxix.

As he spake there of doing, so he speaks here of a certain rule, which he calls, the word of God, whereby all men's works must be squared; for if I do all the works that I can to satisfy another's will or mine own will, it availeth me nothing with God; because I do it not for God. Therefore he which always before followed his own will, when he was stricken down, and began to repent himself, he presently cried out, 'Lord, what wilt thou have me do?' Acts ix.; as if he should say, I will do no more as men would have me, or as the devil would have me, or according as the flesh would have me, but as thou wouldst have me. So David prayed, 'Teach me, O Lord, to do thy will,' not my will; for we need not to be taught to do our own will, no more than a cuckoo to sing *cuckoo*, her own name. Every man can go to hell without a guide.

Here is the rule now ; if you live by it, then you are kin to Christ. As other kindreds go by birth and marriage, so this kindred goeth by faith and obedience. Hearers are but half kin, as it were in a far degree ; but they which hear and do, are called his mother, which is the nearest kindred of all. Therefore if you have the deed, then are you kin indeed ; there is no promise made to hearers, nor to speakers, nor to readers ; but all promises are made to believers or to doers.

Thus have I shewed you Christ preaching, a great press hearing, his friends and kinsmen interrupting, and Christ again withstanding the interruption ; by this you may see what a spite the devil hath to hinder one sermon ; therefore no marvel though he cause so many to be put to silence ; no marvel though he stand so against a learned ministry ; no marvel though he raise up such slanders upon preachers ; no marvel though he write so many books against the Christian government in the church ; no marvel though he make so many non-residents ; no marvel though he ordain so many dumb priests ; for these make him the god of this world ; the devil is afraid that one sermon will convert us, and we are not moved with twenty; so the devil thinketh better of us than we are.

Again, by this you may learn how to withstand temptations; whether it be thy father which tempteth, or thy mother which tempteth, or thy brother which tempteth, or thy sister which tempteth, or thy kinsman which tempteth, or ruler which tempteth, or master which tempteth, or wife which tempteth. As Christ would not know his mother against his Father, so thou shouldst not know any father, or mother, or brother, or sister, or friend, or kinsman, or master, or child, or wife, against God.

If the mother's suit may be refused sometime, a nobleman's letter may be refused too; he that can turn his hindrance to a furtherance, as our Saviour did here, maketh use of everything. Again, by this you may learn how to choose your friends. As Christ counted none his kinsmen, but such as 'hear the word of God, and do it'; so we should make none our familiars, but such as Christ counteth his kinsmen. Again, you may see the difference between Christ and the world; Christ calleth the godly his kinsmen, be they never so poor, and we scorn to call the poor our kinsmen, be they never so honest; so proud is the servant above his Master. Again, by this you see how Christ is to be loved; for when he calleth us his mother, he shews us the way to love him as a mother ; for indeed he is the mother of his mother, and his brethren too. Again, by this, all vaunting and boasting of kindred is cut off. Glory not in that thou hast a gentleman to thy father, glory not that thou hast a knight to thy brother, but glory that thou hast a Lord to thy brother.

Therefore, now we may conclude. You have heard the word ; if you go away and do it, then you are the mother, brethren, and sisters of the heavenly King, to whom, with the Father and the Holy Spirit, be all praise, majesty and dominion, now and evermore. Amen.

THE TRUMPET OF THE SOUL
SOUNDING TO JUDGMENT

Rejoice, O young man, in thy youth, and let thy
heart be merry in thy young days, follow the
ways of thine own heart, and the lusts of thine
eyes : but remember, for all these things thou
must come to judgment.—Eccles. xi. 9.

WHEN I should have preached under the cross,
I mused what text to take in hand, to please all,
and to keep myself out of danger ; and musing,
I could not find any text in the Scripture that did
not reprove sin, unless it were in the Apocrypha,
which is not of the Scripture.   This text bids
them that be voluptuous, be voluptuous still ; let
them that be vainglorious, be vainglorious still ;
let them that be covetous, be covetous still ; let
them that be drunkards, be drunkards still ; let
them that be swearers, be swearers still ; let them
that be wantons, be wantons still ; let them that
be careless prelates, be careless still ; let them
that be usurers, be usurers still ; but, saith
Solomon, ' Remember thy end, that thou shalt be

215

called to judgment at the last for all together.'
This is the counsel of Solomon, the wisest then
living. What a counsel is this for a wise man,
such a one as was Solomon !

In the beginning of his book he saith, 'All is
vanity,' and in the end he saith, ' Fear God, and
keep his commandments ' ; in the twelfth chapter
he saith, ' Remember thy Maker in the days of
thy youth ' ; but here he saith, ' Rejoice, O young
man, in thy youth.' Here he speaketh like an
epicure, which saith, Eat, drink, and be merry ;
here he counsels, and here he mocks ; yet after
the manner of scorners, although they deserved
it in shewing their foolishness ; as in the first of
the Proverbs, ' He laughed at the wicked in
derision ' ; as in the second Psalm, God seeing
us follow our own ways. For when he bids
us pray, we play ; and when he bids us run,
we stand still ; and when he bids us fast, we
feast, and send for vanities to make us sport ;
then he laughs at our destruction. Therefore,
when Solomon giveth a sharp reproof, and maketh
you ashamed in one word, he scoffingly bids you
do it again, like a schoolmaster which beateth his
scholar for playing the truant, he biddeth him
play the truant again. Oh, this is the bitterest
reproof of all. But lest any libertine should misconstrue Solomon, and say, that he bids us be

merry and make much of ourselves, therefore he
shutteth up with a watch-word, and setteth a
bridle before his lips, and reproveth it, as he
speaketh it, before he goeth any further, and
saith, 'But remember that for all these things
thou must come to judgment.'

What a thing is this, to say, *Rejoice*, and then
repent ; what a blank to say, *Take thy pleasure*,
and then *thou shalt come to judgment.* It is as
if he should say, Steal and be hanged, steal and
thou darest ; strangle sin in the cradle, for all the
wisdom in the world will not help thee else ; but
thou shalt be in admiration like dreamers, which
dream strange things, and know not how they
come. He saith, 'Remember judgment.' If thou
remember always, then thou shalt have little list
to sin ; if thou remember this, then thou shalt
have little list to fall down to the devil, though
he would give thee all the world, and the glory
thereof. Solomon saith, the weed groweth from
a weed to a cockle, from a cockle to a bramble,
from a bramble to a brier, from a brier to a thorn ;
lying breeds perjury, perjury breeds haughtiness
of heart, haughtiness of heart breeds contempt,
contempt breeds obstinacy, and brings forth
much evil. And this is the whole progress of sin ;
he groweth from a liar to a thief, from a thief to
a murderer, and never leaveth until he hath

THE SERMONS OF HENRY SMITH

searched all the room in hell, and yet he is never
satisfied; the more he sinneth, the more he
searcheth to sin; when he hath deceived, nay, he
hath not deceived thee; as soon as he hath that
he desireth, he hath not that he desireth.

Pleasure is but a spur, riches but a thorn,
glory but a blast, beauty but a flower; sin is but
an hypocrite, honey in thy mouth and poison in
thy stomach; therefore let us come again and
ask Solomon in good sooth, whether he meaneth
in good earnest, when he spake these words:
Oh, saith Solomon, it is the best life in the world
to go brave, lie soft, and live merrily, if there were
no judgment. But this judgment mars all, it is
like a damp that puts out all the light, and like a
box that marreth all the ointment; for if this be
true, we have spun a fair thread, that we must
answer for all, that are not able to answer for one;
why Solomon maketh us fools, and giveth us
gauds to play withal; what then, shall we not
rejoice at all? Yes, there is a godly mirth, and
if we could hit on it, which is called, 'Be merry
and wise.' Sarah laughed, and was reproved;
Abraham laughed, and was not reproved. And
thus much for the first part.

*But remember, for all these things thou shalt
come to judgment.*

This verse is as it were a dialogue betwixt the

flesh and the spirit, as the two counsellors ; the worst is first, and the flesh speaketh proudly, but the spirit cometh in burdened with that which hath been spoken. The flesh goeth laughing and singing to hell ; but the spirit casteth rubs in his way, and puts him in mind of judgment, that for all these things now ends *rejoice*, and here comes in *but* ; if this *but* were not we might rejoice still. Methinks I see a sword hang in the air by a twine thread, and all the sons of men labour to burst it in sunder. There is a place in hell where the covetous judge sitteth, the greedy lawyer, the griping landlord, the careless bishop, the lusty youth, the wanton dames, the thief, the robbers of the commonwealth.

Now put together *rejoice* and *remember*, thou hast learned to be merry, now learn to be wise. Now therefore, turn over a new leaf and take a new lesson, for now Solomon mocked not as he did before ; therefore a check to thy ruffs, a check to thy cuffs, a check to thy robes, a check to thy gold, a check to your riches, a check to your beauty, a check to your graces.

What ! Do you think that God doth not remember our sins, which we do not regard ; for while we sin, the score runs on, and the judge setteth down all in the table of remembrance, and his scroll reacheth up to heaven.

Item, for lending to usury ; item, for racking
of rents ; item, for deceiving thy brethren ; item,
for falsehood in wares ; item, for starching thy
ruffs ; item, for curling thy hair ; item, for paint-
ing thy face ; item, for selling of benefices ; item,
for starving of souls ; item, for playing at cards ;
item, for sleeping in the church ; item, for pro-
faning the Sabbath day ; with a number more
hath God to call to account, for every one must
answer for himself : the fornicator for taking of
filthy pleasure ; O son, remember thou hast taken
thy pleasure, take thy punishment ; the careless
prelate, for murdering so many thousand souls ;
the landlord, for getting money from his poor
tenants by racking of his rents. See the rest, all
they shall come like a very sheep, when the
trumpet shall sound, and the heaven and earth
shall come to judgment against them ; when the
heavens shall vanish like a scroll, and the earth
shall consume like fire, and all the creatures
standing against them ; the rocks shall cleave
asunder, and the mountains shake, and the
foundation of the earth shall tremble ; and they
shall say to the mountains, Cover us, fall upon us,
and hide us from the presence of his anger and
wrath, whom we have not cared for to offend.

Then Judas would restore his bribes, Esau
would cast up his pottage, Achan would cast

down his gold ; and Gehazi would refuse his gifts, Nebuchadnezzar would be humbler, Balaam would be faithful, and the prodigal would be tame.

Methinks I see Achan running about, Where shall I hide my gold that I have stolen, that it might not be seen, nor stand to appear for a witness against me?

And Judas running to the high priests, saying, Hold, take again your money, I will none of it, I have betrayed the innocent blood.

And Esau, crying for the blessing when it is too late, having sold his birthright for a mess of pottage.

Herod shall then wish that he were John Baptist, Pharaoh would wish that he were Moses, and Saul would wish that he had been David ; Nebuchadnezzar, that he had been Daniel ; Haman, to have been Mordecai ; Esau would wish to be Jacob, and Balaam would wish he might die the death of the righteous ; then he would say, I will give more than Hezekiah, cry more than Esau, fast more than Moses, pray more than Daniel, weep more than Mary Magdalene, suffer more stripes than Paul, abide more imprisonment than Micaiah, abide more cruelty than any mortal man would do, that it might be ; *Ite*, *Go*, *ye cursed*, might be, *Come*, *ye blessed*.

THE SINFUL MAN'S SEARCH

*If thou wilt early seek unto God, and pray unto
the Almighty; if thou be pure and upright;
then surely he will awake unto thee, and make
the habitation of thy righteousness prosperous.
And though thy beginning be but small, yet
thy latter end shall greatly increase.*—Job
viii. 5–7.

IN a sick and evil affected body, dearly beloved,
we usually see preparatives ministered, that the
maladies may be made more fit and pliable to
receive wholesome medicines. The like, yea,
and greater regard ought we to have of our souls,
which not being crazy only, or lightly affected
with sin, but sick even unto death, had need to be
prepared with threats and exhortations, comforts
and consolations, one way or other, that they
may be made fit, not to receive the preparative,
but the perfection of happy salvation. And for
this cause have I made choice of this part of
Scripture, as of a light to shine unto us in darkness, a direction to our steps, and a lantern to
our paths, while we wander through the boisterous

222

waves of this wicked world. The text is plain,
and object to every man's capacity, naturally
budding unto blossoms.

To this end, the word *seeking* is used in this
place, that we may learn, that as the heavens and
the planets, and the whole frame of nature, were
ordained to finish their course by motions and
operation ; so man, as he was ordained to a most
blessed and happy end, should attain thereunto,
not by sloth and idleness, but by an earnest
seeking of the same.

The kingdom of heaven is like a treasure,
which cannot be found without seeking and
digging, Mat. xiii. 44. It is like the precious
pearl, for which the wise merchant was content
not only to seek, but to sell all that he had to
buy it. God hath placed us here in this world as
husbandmen, to plough upon the fallow of our
hearts ; as labourers to work in the vineyard, as
travellers to seek a country, as soldiers to fight
the battle of the Lord, against the flesh, the
world, and the devil.

And for this purpose hath he proposed unto
us an untilled land, a vineyard, a triple enemy to
fight against ; that we might remember, that we
must till the ground, if we will reap the fruit, that
we must prune the vine, if we will drink of the
grape ; that we must fight, if we will overcome.

' He that tilleth the land,' saith the wise man,
' shall be satisfied with bread, but he that followeth
idleness shall be filled with poverty,' Prov. xxviii.
Idleness is a moth or canker of the mind, and
the fruits thereof are wicked cogitations, evil
affections, and worse actions ; corrupt trees without fruit, twice dead, and plucked up by the
roots, engendering in the mind a loathing of God
and godliness.

Fly idleness therefore, and seek virtue, and the
way thereof ; seek learning as for a jewel, make
diligent search and inquisition after her ; seek
early and seek late ; in the morning sow thy
seed, and in the evening let not thy hand rest ;
seek her in the day of trouble, and she will deliver
thee, and thou shalt glorify her.

Seek therefore, and seek early, consecrate
yourselves Nazarites unto the Lord, touch no
unclean thing, give no provocation to the flesh.
Strive with the cock in watchfulness, and rise
with the chirping of the birds, Eccles. xii. ;
sacrifice your body a sweet smelling sacrifice unto
the Lord. This sacrifice is like a sacrifice of
fine flour ; it is like the fat taken from the peace-
offering ; yea, it is better than any sacrifice, it is
like the flower of roses in the spring of the year,
and as the lilies in the springs of water, and as
the branches of frankincense in the time of

summer: And as a vessel of massy gold beset with rich precious stones, as a fair olive that is fruitful, and as the tree that groweth up to the clouds, Ecclus. xxxii., xlvii., l.

Wherefore, to end this point: seek for knowledge as for a treasure, and for wisdom, as for the wedge of gold of Ophir. No mention shall be made in comparison of it, of coral, gabish, or that precious onyx, for 'wisdom is more precious than pearls.' But above all things, seek it where it may be found; and where is the place of understanding? Surely man knoweth not the path thereof. The deep saith, It is not in me; the sea saith, It is not in me; death and destruction say, We have heard the fame thereof with our ears; all creatures say, It is not with us: but God understandeth the way thereof; and unto man he saith, The fear of the Lord is the beginning of wisdom, and to depart from evil is understanding. We are to seek unto God alone, because none is so present as he; for God, because he is Almighty, and with his power filleth both heaven and earth, is present always with them that fear him, and ready to succour them in distress. 'The Lord is near to all that call upon him in truth'; he heareth our groanings and sighs, and knoweth what things are necessary for us before we ask; there is none so willing to help as he. It is a great courage to us to make suit, when we are persuaded of the willingness of him to whom we make suit ; and I pray ye, who was ever more careful for our salvation, and more watchful over us than the Lord ? Who ever put his trust in him, and was confounded ? In this respect he is called a Father, because as the father tendereth his son, so the Lord doth all those that put their trust in him. Can there be any more willing to help us than Christ, whose whole head was sick, and whose heart was heavy for our sakes ? yea, in whose body, from the sole of the foot to the crown of the head, was nothing but wounds, and swellings, and sores ? But, alas, this was nothing to that he suffered for our sakes. He was compassed about with fear and horrors, till his sweat was drops of blood, and his bones bruised in the flesh ; he was whipped, and scourged, and chastised with sorrows, till he cried out in the bitterness of his soul, 'O Lord, if it be possible, let this cup pass from me.' The heavy hand of God was so grievous upon him, that he bruised his very bones, and rent his reins asunder ; he could find no health in his flesh, but was wounded, yea, wounded to the death, even the most bitter death upon the cross. His tender fingers were nailed to the cross ; his face was wrinkled with weeping and wailing ; his sides imbrued and gored with his own blood, spurting and gushing fresh from his ribs ; the shadow of death was upon his eyes.

Having spoken of the search, it followeth that I speak of the manner how it is to be made. In prayer, by these words, *If thou pray unto the Almighty*.

I shewed you before the force of our adversary ; receive now a shield against his force, even the shield of prayer. He is not to be resisted by ringing of an hallowed bell, nor by sprinkling of holy water, nor by the relics of saints, nor by our own works and merits.

Oh sure fortress, more forcible than any engine, and stronger than the gates of hell; and to conclude the sum and substance of all in few words, the only thing whereby mortal men have the clouds, and the stars, and the angels, and all the powers of heaven at commandment. For as Deborah sung in her song, 'They fought from heaven, even the stars in their courses fought against Sisera.' For all creatures have been subject to the prayers of the faithful to revenge the Lord's quarrel, to 'help the Lord, to help the Lord against the mighty.' Prayer hath ever been the cognisance, and the victory, and the triumph of the faithful, for as the soul giveth life to the body, so prayer giveth life to the soul.

Oh that I could engrave the love of it in your

hearts, as with a diamond, and so instil your minds, that my words might be pricks to your consciences, and thereby give you occasion to pray often. It is a wonderful matter to be able to persuade men ; but if prayer be able to persuade the living God, oh how great is the force thereof, it goeth through the clouds, and ceaseth not till it come near, and will not depart until the Most High have respect thereunto. Oh that you would therefore pray often, and learn of Christ (the most absolute pattern of our life) to pray continually. He prayed in his baptism, in the wilderness, in preaching, in working of miracles, in his passion on the mount, in the garden, in his last supper, in commending his spirit to God at all times and in all places, that he might leave unto us an example of the same. It followeth, *And pray to the Almighty*.

Puttest thou any trust in man, whose breath is in his nostrils? Cursed is he that maketh man his strength, and flesh his arm. Surely Pharaoh, and all princes, are ' a broken staff, on which, if a man lean, it will strike into his hand and pierce it,' and lay him grovelling in the dust. 'It is better, therefore, to trust in the Lord, than to put any confidence in princes.'

The second thing we have to note in his promises, is his mercy, which exceedeth all his

228

works. For God, though he hath given a curse of the law against sinners, yet seeing Christ for the penitent hath borne the curse, whereby his justice is not impaired, he is content to accept our weakness as our strength, to recompense our imperfection with reward of greatest perfection ; and that which we can perform but in small part, he is content to accept as whole, not for any desert of ours, but in satisfaction of his Son, who paid with the seal of his own blood, the ransom for our sins, he hath cancelled the hand-writing that was against us. Wherefore we are to pray unto God, that whensoever our sins shall come in question before him, that he would look upon Christ Jesus, the true looking-glass, in whom he shall find us most pure and innocent, and to shine most clearly in the righteousness which he hath given us by faith ; so that we appear not in our own righteousness, but in the righteousness of the Lamb, who having taken away the sins of the world, and having made us as white as snow, though we were as red as crimson, saith, he will be merciful to our iniquities, and will remember our sins no more. Of him do all the prophets bear witness, that 'through his name all that believe shall receive remission of their sins.' Again, ' Drink ye all of this, for this is my blood which is shed for the remission of sins.' Christ

gave himself for our sins, that he might deliver us
from the curse of the law, even according to the
will of the Father. Christ 'bare our sins in his
own body on the tree, that we being delivered
from sin, might live in righteousness, by whose
stripes we are healed, for we were as sheep going
astray, but are now returned to the shepherd and
bishop of our souls.' It is no more but believe
and be saved ; believe and receive remission ;
believe, and lay off thine own righteousness, and
invest thyself with the righteousness of the
unspotted Lamb.

Lastly, for being pure and upright, he will
make thy latter end greatly increase, and, that
thou mayest the less mistrust his promises, he
will do it though thy beginning be but small.

Here, brethren, ye see what a sea of matter is
offered me, whereunto, if I would commit myself,
I might discourse unto you what strange events,
by God's providence, have happened in the world,
what great kings and potentates have been
plucked down from their thrones, and what
contemptible persons in the eyes of the world
have been advanced to their rooms : how
Mordecai, a stranger, was exalted into Haman's
place, Esther viii. ; how Joseph and Daniel, the
one a bondman in Egypt, the other a captive in
Babylon, were made princes in those kingdoms,

Gen. xli., Dan. vi. But because I will not over-much transgress the bounds of modesty, or hold you longer than in this place I have been accustomed, only remember what the prophet saith, ' He raiseth the needy out of the dust, and lifteth the poor out of the mire, that he might set him with the princes, even with princes of the world,' Ps. cxiii. 5.

Remember the example of David, whom the Lord chose and took from the ewes great with young, that he might feed his people in Jacob, and his inheritance in Israel, Ps. lxxviii. Remember the example of Job, how the Lord turned the captivity of Job, as the rivers of the south ; how he blessed the last days of Job more than the first ; how he gave him sheep, and camels, and oxen, and she-asses in more abundance than he had before ; how he increased him with sons and daughters, even to the fourth generation, so that he died being old and full of days, Job xlii. Remember even our own estate, for whom the Lord hath done great things already ; hath created us, and redeemed us, and sanctified us, and not long since delivered us from the gaping jaws of those that sought to suck our blood. Upon some he hath bestowed humility, whereby their minds are adorned with virtue ; honour upon others, whereby their persons are invested with majesty; upon others comeliness, whereby the other two are graced; upon others orchards, which they planted not, at least into which they gave no increase; upon others, increase of virtuous children, whereby their posterity is preserved; upon others, the free passage of his word, which a long time had been obscured by ignorance, the mother of devotion, as the shavelings call it, but rather a stepdame of destruction, as we perceive it; and though he bestow but some one or two of his blessings upon us, yet how much are we bound for these blessings to sing praise, and honour, and glory, unto him that sitteth upon the throne, and unto the Lamb for ever. But upon whom he hath bestowed all these blessings, oh how strictly by good cause are they bound to magnify the Lord, and to rejoice in God their Saviour. Examine then your own consciences, I beseech you, whether God hath bestowed all these blessings upon you, or no; and if he have, oh what great cause have you to come before his face with praise, to sing loud unto him with psalms, to worship and to fall down before him, to give unto the Lord the glory of his name, to bring an offering of thanksgiving, and to enter into his courts with praise. And yet who knoweth whether the Lord hath greater blessings for you in store? Ye may be sure he will pull down the mighty from their seat, and exalt the humble and meek. Surely the Lord doth use virtue as a means to bring us to honour, and whosoever you shall see endued with the virtues of this text, I mean with seeking unto God with prayer and purity of life, ye may be sure there is a blessing reserved for him of the Lord, yea, such a blessing, as though his beginning be but small, yet his latter end shall greatly increase.

God increase the love of these things in our hearts, and make us worthy of Christ's blessings, which he hath plentifully in store for us; that after he hath heaped temporal blessings upon us, he will give us the blessing of all blessings, even the life of the world to come.

MARY'S CHOICE

*Now it came to pass, as they went, that he
entered into a certain town: and a certain
woman, named Martha, received him into
her house. Now she had a sister called Mary,
which also sat at Jesus' feet, and heard his
preaching. But Martha was cumbered about
much serving, and came to him, and said,
Master, dost thou not care that my sister hath
left me to serve alone? bid her therefore that
she help me. And Jesus answered and said
unto her, Martha, Martha, thou carest and
art troubled about many things. But one
thing is needful; Mary hath chosen the good
part which shall not be taken away from her.*
—Luke x. 38–42.

OH happy house, that entertained such a
guest! but thrice happy inhabitants, to whom
such a guest would vouchsafe to come! When
he came to the swinish Gadarenes, they desired
him to depart out of their coasts, preferring their
swine above their Saviour, Luke viii.; but this

234

godly family received him into their houses,
preferring their God before their gold, and the
health of souls before their worldly wealth. They
received him into their house, who had not a
house wherein to put his head, Mat. viii. 19,
wherein their hospitality is commended, and shall
certainly be rewarded at the dreadful day; for
with this and such like works of mercy, the Lord
shall answer the sentence of judgment, which is
to be denounced against the wicked, that never
exercised those works of mercy.

Let us learn by their example to be harbourers,
and given to hospitality, which is so often commended unto us in the Scripture, and shall be
so richly rewarded at the last day. Those godly
fathers, Abraham and Lot, entertained angels
in the habit of strangers, Gen. xviii. and xix.; so
we may duly entertain Christ Jesus in the habit
of a poor man, of a blind man, or of a lame man;
and whatsoever is done to any of these that are
his members, he accounteth and accepteth as
done unto himself.

When Martha had thus entertained Christ, as
he was man, into her house, Mary began to
entertain him, as he was God, into her heart; she
sat at his feet to hear his preaching; for no
sooner was Christ come into the house, but that
he took occasion to teach and to instruct the

family; and instead of bodily food, which they bestowed upon him, to give unto them the food of the soul. Thus doth he always shew himself a thankful guest, into what house soever he entereth; he leaveth better things behind him than he findeth. He loves not to be in Zacchæus's debt for his dinner, for instead thereof he bringeth salvation to his house, Luke xix.; neither doth he leave his supper unpaid for here, for instead thereof he bestoweth upon them an heavenly sermon. This should be the exercise of faithful ministers, when they are invited to great feasts, that as they are called the salt of the earth, Mat. v. 13, which serveth to season the meats, to make them savoury, and preserve them from putrefaction, so they should season the table-talk with some godly conference, to minister grace unto the hearers, Eph. iv. 29.

These sisters were godly women, and both earnest favourers of Jesus Christ, and yet in the manner of their devotion there is such difference, that the worldly affection of the one may in some sort be misliked, in respect of the godly exercise and practice of the other. Martha is sore encumbered with much serving, where a little service had been sufficient; but Mary is attentive to hear the word of God, which never can be heard sufficiently.

MARY'S CHOICE

Mary sitteth to hear the word, as Christ used to sit when he preached the word, Mat. v., Luke iv., John viii., to shew that the word is to be preached and heard with a quiet mind. In a still night every voice is heard, and when the body is quiet, the mind most commonly is quiet also. But Martha is troubled with other affairs, and therefore unfit to hear the word, as the ground that is surcharged with stones, or overgrown with weeds and thorns, is unfit to receive the seed, or yield any fruit to him that tilleth it. As often therefore as we come to hear the word of God, we must not come with distracted minds, we must not trouble ourselves with the cares of this life, which, as our Saviour said, are thorns to choke the word, and to make it unfruitful. For Moses was unfit to talk with God, till he had put off his shoes, Exod. iii., and the blind man unfit to come to Christ, till he had thrown away his cloak, Mat. x. ; so we must think ourselves unfit to hear the word, and unapt for every heavenly exercise, till we have put off our shoes, that is, our worldly cogitations and affections.

Thus in Christ we have the patience of a good pastor, and in Mary the pattern of a good hearer. Let ministers learn by his example to take all occasions to preach the word, to be instant in season and out of season, 2 Tim. iv. 2 ;

and let Christians learn by her example, first, to seek the kingdom of God and his righteousness, and then to provide for the things of this life, Mat. vi.

While Mary was careful for the food of the soul, Martha was curious to provide food for the body ; her greatest care was to entertain Christ, and to make him good cheer, to testify her thankful mind unto him that had done so great things for them : he had raised her brother Lazarus from death to life ; therefore he was worthy to be well entertained.

It was well done therefore of Martha to shew her thankful mind unto Christ, but it was not well done *at that time* to shew herself thankful *in that manner* ; it was then time to hear the word, for at that time Christ preached the word ; it was no time for her to spend that time in other affairs, and to neglect the greatest affairs, the means of her own salvation.

It was not unlawful for Martha to labour on, more than it was unlawful for Peter to sleep, Mat. xxv. ; but when Christ was preaching, it was no time for her to be so busy in serving, no more than it was time for Peter to sleep when Christ willed him so earnestly to watch and pray. When Christ preached out of Simon's ship to the people that stood upon the shore, Luke v., it was no time for Peter to play the fisherman. But when Christ had left speaking, and commanded him to launch into the deep, then it was time for Peter to let down the net.

There is a time wherein we ought to labour in our vocation, and a time wherein we ought to hear the word ; and as we may not utterly neglect our lawful callings to follow sermons, so must not we bestow the Sabbath, which is consecrated to the service of God, in following the works of our vocation. All things have their appointed time, saith the wise man, Eccles. iii., and everything is seemly in his convenient season ; but when things are done preposterously and out of order, there followeth confusion.

The repetition of Martha's name argueth the vehemency and earnestness of this admonition. The Lord is fain to be very earnest and importunate with us, before he can reclaim us. So when God spake unto Abraham, he called him twice by name ; Christ called Peter thrice by name, John xxi., to cause him to make his threefold confession, to make amends for his threefold denial. And when the Lord spake unto Samuel, he called him four several times by name before he answered, for such is the great mercy of God, that he is content to admonish us often of our duty ; and such is the dulness and perverseness

239

of our crooked nature, that we cannot be gained by the first admonition ; but the Lord must call us often and earnestly, before we will hearken unto him.

There are two things in the speech of Christ to be observed : the first is, his modest reprehension of Martha's immoderate care ; the other is, his friendly defence of Mary's choice. Though Martha was very careful to entertain Christ in the best manner, yet if he perceive anything in her worthy reprehension, he will not stick to tell her of it ; he will not soothe her in her saying, nor smoothe her in her own conceit, for all the trouble and cost that she bestows upon him. If we be often invited to some man's table, and kindly entertained, it would be unkindly taken if we should find fault with any disorder ; but forasmuch as all Christ his actions are the instructions of Christians, therefore every Christian, but especially preachers, whom it more specially concerneth, must learn by this example how to behave themselves, when they are invited to great feasts, namely, speak their conscience freely when they see a fault. The best requital that we can make for our good cheer, is to give good counsel and wholesome admonitions to them that invite us.

Thus is Martha reprehended for her curiosity ;

now let us see how Mary is excused, and commended for her godly care. One thing is necessary, saith Christ; and what is that one thing? Even to hear the word preached, which is the power of God to salvation, to every one that believeth. A man may better want all things than that one needful thing; and yet we desire all other things, and neglect that one thing, which is so needful.

This one thing hath Mary chosen, and therefore hath chosen the better part. Martha's part is good, because it provideth for this present life; but Mary's part is better, because it leadeth to eternal life. It is good to be occupied about our calling, to get our living; but it is better to be occupied in hearing the word, which is able to save our souls. As the head and the foot are both needful in the body, so Mary and Martha are both needful in a commonwealth; man hath two vocations, the one earthly by his labour, the other heavenly by his prayer. There is the active life, which consisteth in practising the affairs of this life, wherein man sheweth himself to be like himself; and there is the contemplative life, which consisteth in the meditation of divine and heavenly things, wherein man sheweth himself to be like the angels; for they which labour in their temporal vocations, do live like men;

but they which labour in spiritual matters, live like angels. When they hear the word, God speaketh unto them ; when they pray, they speak unto God ; so that there is a continual conference between God and them, because they are continually exercised in hearing and praying.

Christ loved Martha for her hospitality, as Isaac loved Esau for his venison. So did he love Mary for diligence in hearing his word, as Rebekah loved Jacob for hearkening to her voice. A nurse which hath her breast full of milk, doth love the child that sucks it from her ; and Christ which hath his breast full of heavenly milk, is glad when he hath children to suck the same ; let us therefore, as the apostle willeth us, 1 Pet. ii. 12, 'laying aside all maliciousness, and all guile, and dissimulation, and envy, and all evil speaking, as new born babes, desire the sincere milk of the word, that we may grow thereby,' to be perfect men in Christ Jesus. Let us breathe after the fountain of the living water, which springeth up into eternal life ; and as the fainty hart desireth the water-brook to quench his thirst, Ps. xlii. 1. And forasmuch as many things are so troublesome, and one thing is so needful, let us seek that one needful thing, the end of all things, even to fear God and keep his commandments.

EPISTLE DEDICATORY

To my late Auditors, the Congregation of Clement
Danes, all the good will which I can wish.

BELOVED in Christ Jesus, my first fruits, I have
nothing but this mite to leave with you, which is
the sum of all my sermons. Ye have heard it
already; and as the apostle calls the Corinthians
his epistle, 2 Cor. iii. 2, so ye should be my
sermon; that is, my sermon should be printed in
your hearts, as this is printed in paper. If you
have not given your hearts to him that sent for
them, now think that God hath sent for them
again, and hear me writing, whom ye cannot hear
speaking. Take not custom for religion; shun
occasion as well as sin; seek the use of everything; desire not to have your kingdom here.
And so I leave you all with Christ, whom I have
preached, to bring forth the fruit of that seed
which is sown, beseeching you for all the love
that you have of heaven, that ye would not count
anything in this world worthy to keep your hearts
from God, but think of the day when ye shall

give account for every sermon which ye have heard; and he which hath called you in this prison will glorify you in his palace, where ye shall see him to whom ye have given your hearts, and enjoy that blessing of blessings which makes all the world to worship him. The Father of our Lord Jesus Christ, which hath begun to draw you to his kingdom, never leave you until you come unto it. Amen.

Your late unworthy servant for the Lord,

H. S.

THE CHRISTIAN'S SACRIFICE

My son, give me thy heart.—Prov. xxiii. 26.

To bind all the lessons together which ye have learned since I came, this sentence came unto my mind, 'My son, give me thy heart,' which is the sum of all that ye have heard, and shews in what chest you should lay up these treasures in your heart, and then give that heart to God and he will keep all safe.

A supplication is come as it were from God to man, that man would send God his heart. He which always gave now craves, and he which craves always now gives. Christ stands at the door like a poor man, and asks not bread, nor clothes, nor lodgings, which we should give to his members, but our heart, that is, even the continent of all, and governor of man's house, which sits on the bench like a judge to give the charge, and teacheth the tongue to speak, the hand to work, the foot to walk, the ear to attend, the eye to observe, the mind to choose, and the flesh to obey. That we must present to God, like

245

a burnt-sacrifice, wherein all is offered together, Lev. i. 9, a wise tongue, a diligent hand, a wary foot, a watchful eye, an attentive ear, an humble mind, an obedient flesh, put all together, and it is but the heart : 'My son,' saith God, 'give me thy heart.' Here thou art a giver, God the petitioner, thy heart the gift which he claimeth by the name of a son.

Mark what God hath chosen for himself : not that which any other should lose by, like the demands of them which care for none but themselves, but that which, being given to God, moves us to give unto every man his due.

Once God required offerings and sacrifices which men were unwilling to give, because it was a dear service of God, Mal. i. 13, and iii. 13 ; but now he saith that the heart is more than all burnt-offerings and sacrifices, Mark xii. 33. Jacob loved Joseph more than all his brethren, Gen. xxxvii., so God loveth the heart more than all her fellows ; this mite God will have for all his benefits, which we may best afford him. Thy alms to the poor, thy counsel to the simple, thy inheritance to thy children, thy tribute to Cæsar, but thy heart to God ; he which is a Spirit requires a spirit, John iv. 24, and delights to dwell in the hearts of men. Here God plants himself, as in a castle which is always besieged with the world, the flesh, and the devil. If the enemy get a thought, or a word, or a work, yet he hath but razed the walls ; but if he take the heart, then the fortress is lost. For that time all our thoughts, words, and works are captive unto him : he bids them go, and they go ; do, and they do it.

As a man considers what he doth when he gives, so God licenseth us to consider of that which we do for him, whether he deserves it, whether we owe it, whether he can require it, lest it should come against our will ; therefore *give me*, saith God, as though he would not strain upon us or take from us ; but if thou wilt give him thy heart, then he accepts it ; it must come freely like a gift, as his blessings come to us, and then his demand is granted. Here is no respect of time, how long thou mayest stay it, or how long he will keep it ; but give it, is the present time ; as though he would have it out of hand while he asketh, before ye go out of the church ; for what can we ask of him, when we deny him but one thing when he asks of us? Therefore consider who is a suitor to you, and let all suitors have their answer, that thy heart is married already. As Isaac answered Esau, ' Jacob have I blessed, and he shall be blessed,' Gen. xxvii., so thou mayest say, God hath my heart, and he shall have it ; and them that crave it hereafter, send them to Christ for it, for it is not thine to give, if thou hast given it to God already. But take heed thy heart do not lie to thyself, and say it is God's when it is the world's ; like Jeroboam's wife, which would not seem to be Jeroboam's wife, 1 Kings xiv. 2. By this thou shalt know whether thou hast given it to him or no ; if the heart be gone, all will follow. As the sun riseth first, and then the beasts arise from their dens, the fowls from their nests, and men from their beds ; so when the heart sets forward to God, all the members will follow after it, the tongue will praise him, the foot will follow him, the ear will attend him, the eye will watch him, the hand will serve him, nothing will stay after the heart, but every one goes, like handmaids after their mistress.

This is the melody which Paul speaketh of : Eph. v. 19, 'Make melody to the Lord in your hearts' ; shewing, that there is a concert of all the members when the heart is in tune, and that it sounds like a melody in the ears of God, and makes us rejoice while we serve him. We have example hereof in Christ, which said it was meat and drink unto him to do his Father's will, John iv. 34 ; and in David, which danced to see the ark, 2 Sam. vi. 14 ; and in the Israelites, of whom it is said, that they rejoiced when they offered from their heart unto the Lord, 1 Chron. xxix. 9.

Therefore Solomon, picking out the heart for God, spake as though he would set out the pleasantest, and fairest, and easiest way to serve him, without any grudging, or toil, or weariness. Touch but the first link, all the rest will follow ; so set the heart a-going, and it is like the poise of a clock, which turns all the wheels one way. Such an oil is upon the heart, which makes all nimble and current about it ; therefore it is almost as easy to speak well, and do well, as to think well. If the heart indite a good matter, no marvel though the tongue be the pen of a ready writer, Ps. xlv. 1, but if the heart be dull, all is like a left hand, so unapt and untoward, that it cannot turn itself to any good.

As Joseph charged his brethren that they should not come to him for corn unless they brought Benjamin unto him, whom they left at home, Gen. xlii. 15, Mark xv. 8, so God will not have us to speak to him, nor come to him for anything, unless we bring our hearts unto him, which we leave behind. The tongue without the heart is a flattering tongue ; the eye without the heart is a wicked eye ; the ear without the heart is a vain ear ; the hand without the heart is a false hand. Dost thou think that God will accept

249

a flattering tongue, a wicked eye, a vain ear, a false hand, which rejecteth a sacrifice if it be but lean or bruised? No, saith Paul, in his first epistle to the Corinthians, Chap. xiii. ver. 1, 'If I give all that I have, and not love,' that is, give not my heart, 'it avails me nothing.' He saith not, that they which give not their heart give nothing, but that they shall have nothing for such offerings. He which brings but a mite, and brings his heart, brings more than he which offers a talent, Mark xii. 42 ; and he shall go away more justified than he which said, 'All these have I kept from my youth upward,' Mat. xix. 20 ; for God is not mocked, Gal. vi. 7, but knows how much is behind, though Ananias seem to bring all, Acts v. 3. He marks how I speak, and how you hear, and how we pray in this place ; and if it come not from the heart, he repels it as fast as it goes up, like the smoke which climbs towards heaven, but never comes there. Man thinks when he hath the gift, he hath the heart too ; but God, when he hath the gift, calls for the heart still, Ps. lxxiii. 1. The pharisee's prayer, the harlot's vow, the traitor's kiss, the sacrifice of Cain, the feast of Jezebel, the oblations of Ananias, the tears of Esau, are nothing to him, but still he cries, Bring thy heart, or bring nothing ; like a jealous husband, when he hath a wife, yet he is jealous whether he hath her heart or no, so, whatsoever thou do, yet God is jealous still, and respects not what thou dost, but whether thou do it from thy heart; that is, of mere love toward him. If Pilate had washed his heart when he washed his hands, Mat. xxvii. 24, he had been cleaner than Naaman when he came out of Jordan, 2 Kings v. 13.

Of all the suitors which come unto you, it seems there is none which hath any title to claim the heart but God, which challengeth it by the name of a son, Mal. i. 8, as if he should say, Thou shalt give it to thy Father which gave it to thee : art thou my son? My sons give me their hearts, and by this they know that I am their Father, if I dwell in their hearts, for the heart is the temple of God, 1 Cor. vi. 16; therefore, if thou be his son, thou wilt give him thy heart, because thy Father desires it, thy Maker desires it, thy Redeemer desires it, thy Saviour desires it ; thy Lord, and thy King, and thy Master desires it, which hath given his Son for a ransom, his Spirit for a pledge, his word for a guide, the world for a walk, and reserves a kingdom for thine inheritance. Canst thou deny him anything, which hath given the heir for the servant, his beloved for his enemy, the best for the worst? Rom. viii. 32. Canst thou

251

deny him anything, whose goodness created us, whose favour elected us, whose mercy redeemed us, whose wisdom converteth us, whose grace preserved us, whose glory shall glorify us? Oh, if thou knewest, as Christ said to the woman of Samaria when she huckt to give him water, John iv. 10, 'If thou knewest who it is that saith unto thee,' Give me thy heart, thou wouldst say unto him, as Peter did when Christ would wash his feet, John xiii. 9, 'Lord, not my feet only, but my hands and my head'; not my heart only, but all my body, and my thoughts, and my words, and my works, and my goods, and my life, take all that thou hast given.

If Abraham gave Lot leave to choose what part he did like, Gen. xiii. 8, 9, shall we not give God leave to choose that which he liketh? If he did not love thee, he would not require thy heart; for they which love, require the heart. The master requires labour, the landlord requires service, the captain requires fight; but he that requires the heart, requires it for love, for the heart is love. We will give him little, if we will not give him that which he asks for love towards ourselves.

Thus ye have heard what God requires for all that he hath given you, and how all your services are lost until you bring it. What shall I wish

252

you now before my departure? I wish you would give all your hearts to God while I speak, that ye might have a kingdom for them. Send for your hearts where they are wandering, one from the bank, another from the tavern, another from the shop, another from the theatres ; call them home, and give them all to God, and see how he will welcome them, as the father embraceth the son, Luke xv. 22. If your hearts were with God, durst the devil fetch them? Durst those sins come at them? Even as Dinah was deflowered when she strayed from home, Gen. xxxiv. 2, so is the heart when it strayeth from God. Therefore call thy members together, and let them fast, like a quest of twelve men, until they consent upon the law, before any more terms pass, to give God his right ; and let him take the heart which he wooeth, which he would marry, which he would endow with all his goods, and make it the heir of the crown. When you pray, let your heart pray ; when you hear, let your heart hear ; when you give, let your heart give ; whatsoever you do, set the heart to do it, Prov. iii. 1 ; and if it be not so perfect as it should or ought to be, yet it shall be accepted for the friend that gives it, Dan. x. 12.

I have but one day more to teach you all that you must learn of me, therefore I would hold you here until you assent to give all your hearts to

253

God. If ye give them not now, where have I cast the seed? and how have you heard all this year? If ye will give them now, ye shall be adopted this day the sons of God, and I shall leave you in the bosom of Christ, which will give you heaven for your hearts. The Lord Jesus grant that my words be not the savour of death unto any soul here, 2 Cor. ii. 16, but that you may go in strength thereof through prosperity and adversity, till you hear that comfort from heaven, 'Come, ye blessed, and receive the inheritance prepared for you.'